THE PSYCHOLOGY OF TRUST

What makes us trust people? How is trust developed and maintained? Is Western society facing a crisis of trust?

The Psychology of Trust addresses trust issues that are directly relevant to peoples' experiences in their daily lives. It identifies the factors that cause people to trust, and the consequences of trust for real world issues in health, politics, terrorism, the workplace, and religious faith. It also explores the impact of a lack of trust, and what causes distrust of individuals, groups and organisations.

In a world where trust impacts our daily lives, *The Psychology of Trust* shows the role trust plays in our relationships, and provides practical guidance regarding our own trust in others.

Ken J. Rotenberg is Professor of Psychology at the University of Keele, UK. He has been an active researcher for over 40 years, with a particular interest in trust in childhood and adolescence.

THE PSYCHOLOGY OF EVERYTHING

The Psychology of Everything is a series of books which debunk the myths and pseudo-science surrounding some of life's biggest questions.

The series explores the hidden psychological factors that drive us, from our sub-conscious desires and aversions, to the innate social instincts handed to us across the generations. Accessible, informative, and always intriguing, each book is written by an expert in the field, examining how research-based knowledge compares with popular wisdom, and illustrating the potential of psychology to enrich our understanding of humanity and modern life.

Applying a psychological lens to an array of topics and contemporary concerns – from sex to addiction to conspiracy theories – *The Psychology of Everything* will make you look at everything in a new way.

Titles in the series:

For further information about this series please visit www.thepsychologyofeverything.co.uk

THE PSYCHOLOGY OF TRUST

KEN J. ROTENBERG

Routledge
Taylor & Francis Group

LONDON AND NEW YORK

First published 2018
by Routledge
2 Park Square, Milton Park, Abingdon, Oxon OX14 4RN

and by Routledge
711 Third Avenue, New York, NY 10017

Routledge is an imprint of the Taylor & Francis Group, an informa business

British Library Cataloguing-in-Publication Data
A catalogue record for this book is available from the British Library

Library of Congress Cataloging-in-Publication Data
A catalog record for this book has been requested

ISBN: 978-1-138-67848-4 (hbk)
ISBN: 978-1-138-67849-1 (pbk)
ISBN: 978-1-315-55891-2 (ebk)

Typeset in Joanna
by Apex CoVantage, LLC

CONTENTS

ACKNOWLEDGMENTS

I would like to thank my wife, Carole, for her wonderful support during the writing of this book. This book is dedicated to her.

This book also is dedicated to my son (David), my stepchildren (Claire and Gemma) and my stepgrandchildren (Amber, Lucas Jack, Jessica, and Ruby).

The book also is dedicated to Dr. Lucy Betts who has been a valued colleague in our research and writings on trust. Her competence and dedication is greatly appreciated. Finally, I want to express my appreciation for the support I have received for my work on trust by my colleague Professor Pamela Qualter.

1

UNDERSTANDING TRUST
A crisis or everything?

Authors from many disciplines and across the world have held the position that trust is the cornerstone of society and essential to its survival. This view has been espoused in the disciplines of philosophy (O'Hara, 2004), political science (Uslander, 2002), sociology (Misztal, 1996), and psychology (Rotenberg, 2010; Rotter, 1980). Trust between individuals of different cultures (cross-cultural trust) has been viewed as fundamental to the survival of multicultural societies (Misztal, 1996; Uslander, 2002). The importance of trust highlights the danger posed by the reported growing lack of trust in contemporary society.

A chorus of writers has expressed the proposition that trust is in crisis in contemporary society. Guided by his findings based on his Trust Barometer, Richard Edelman (2015) has asserted, "For the first time since the Great Recession, half the countries we survey have fallen into the 'distruster' category" (n.p.). He argued that this was due to the "failure of key institutions to provide answers or leadership in response to events such as the refugee crisis, data breaches, China's stock market downturn, Ebola in west Africa, the invasion of Ukraine, the FIFA bribery scandal, VW's manipulation of emissions data, massive corruption at Petrobras, and exchange-rate manipulation by the world's largest banks" (n.p.). According to the public media, Britain "is suffering a huge loss of faith in its institutions: Trust in all politicians has slumped to an all-time low" (Slack, 2016, n.p.). Also, survey studies report that the trust of the American people has decreased across the last decade (Zizumbo-Colunga, Zechmeister, & Seligso, 2010). Academic research has not escaped the "crisis" of trust and there are reports that a substantial number of findings presented in journals are inaccurate and biased (see Walia, 2015).

The bulk of support for the idea of trust in crisis is derived from surveys in popular forums that typically assess general views. The findings from surveys are questionable, but they serve the dual function of expressing public concern about trust (i.e., anxiety regarding it) and shaping public opinion regarding trust. The survey findings convey a simple message to a waiting public: *Trust is in crisis and it is on the decline!* Implicit in the survey reports is the notion that the world has become more corrupt and untrustworthy. It is very difficult to confirm or deny that conclusion, because of lack of evidence. It is fair to say that corruption and untrustworthiness have been present throughout the course of human history (Machiavelli testified to this in the late 1400s). What is clear is that access to information revealing people's untrustworthiness is greater than at any time in human history. Because of technology and social media every action is conveyed to millions of people – in the blink of an eye – and is held up for public scrutiny. This change has resulted in an unequalled opportunity for critical evaluation of peoples' behaviour, the detection of untrustworthiness, and the expression of lack of trust in others – especially regarding those individuals in the public eye.

The emphasis on "crises" in trust unfortunately diverts our attention from the notion that trust is essential to day-to-day social interaction and the formation and maintenance of interpersonal relationships (see Rotenberg, 2010). From my perspective, trust is analogous to dark matter in the physical universe. Dark matter is an extensive but difficult-to-detect substance that binds planets and terrestrial material. Similarly, trust is a prevalent but often silent force that connects people and ensures social relationships and social functioning in modern society. I am certain, that without it, our social "universe" would not exist.

The preceding may seem like a bold assertion but careful consideration shows that even the simplest social acts involve trust. For example, I went for lunch in the university building the other day. I bought American street food and a bottle of fizzy drink. There were no food trays so I placed my drink on the counter while I took my American street food to a table around the corner. When I returned to the counter, I found that my drink had been taken. Perhaps one of the thirsty new students who was milling about took it; one will never know. In this situation, I had trusted others both by beliefs and action not to steal my drink. Sadly, that was violated. Nevertheless, I walked off without my drink at the food register in that same building the very next day. The student next to me in line drew my attention to my drink as I was leaving, and I got it. My trust was renewed – although my problem for ensuring that I collect my drink likely remains. The point here is that there are millions of day-to-day social acts that involve trust. Once trust is properly conceptualised and we sidestep the crisis view of it then we come to understand the overwhelming prevalence of trust in our social world. It is not necessary to assert that trust is in crisis to view it as worthy of investigation – although the crisis view may spur on that activity. Let us begin at the beginning, though, by asking the question regarding what trust is. Dictionary definitions are a beginning.

POPULAR DEFINITIONS OF TRUST

The use of the word "trust" in common discourse dates back to the 13th century, in Middle English. It is regarded as probably being of Scandinavian origin, akin to Old Norse *traust* (trust); akin to Old English *trēowe* (faithful) (Merriam-Webster dictionary). The word "trust" dates back much earlier, though, when considered in the context of religion. Trust in God is found both in the Old and New Testaments (Benner, 2004) as well as the Koran. In current times, the religious use of trust is demonstrated in the phrase "In God We Trust", which is the official motto of the US and appears on much of its currency (see Chapter 11).

Aside from the trusts found in banking and financing, "trust" is defined in dictionaries as a "belief that someone or something is reliable, good, effective etc." (Merriam-Webster dictionary) and "to believe that someone is good and honest and will not harm you, or that something is safe and reliable" (Cambridge English dictionary). This book will focus on trust in *someone* as part of the domain of interpersonal trust. Also, research addressing self-trust was excluded for practical reasons. The term "interpersonal" is omitted from the text for brevity.

Elements of popular definitions of trust are (quite correctly) found in academic conceptualisations of trust. It is important to highlight that the conceptualisation of trust in academic writings varies considerably according to the theory, framework, model, or approach adopted by a researcher. This very fact contributes to the problems that researchers with different approaches have in engaging with each other's concepts. These differences contribute to divergence in deciding whether or not the study and findings are accepted by the academic community and publishable. In that context, I will now describe the different approaches to the investigation of trust.

APPROACHES TO THE INVESTIGATION OF TRUST

Psychosocial Theory

Erikson's (1963) Psychosocial Theory is regarded as one of the origins of contemporary psychology. This theory is the most commonly cited account of trust in introductory and developmental psychology texts. The theory posits that development is composed of a sequence of eight stages of psychosocial development. Each stage entails a conflict that can be resolved in a psychologically healthy or unhealthy fashion. The resolution at one stage affects the capacity of the individual to resolve subsequent stages in the sequence. The first is the "Trust vs Mistrust" stage, which occurs from birth to 18 months of age. According to Erikson (1963), during that period, trust is an emotion that comprises an infant's experiential state of confidence that he or she is valued and his or her needs will be met. If the infant encounters that warmth/nurturance from his or her caregiver then he or she attains a basic trust. By contrast, if the infant encounters a lack of warmth/rejection then he or she attains a basic mistrust. The infant who attains basic trust is able to delay gratification and exert control over his or her bodily functions (e.g., bowels). According to this theory the emotion of trust during infancy profoundly affects the course of development.

Attachment Theory

Bowlby (1980) and others such as Ainsworth (e.g., Ainsworth, 1989) have advanced Attachment Theory. According to this theory, infants form different qualities of attachment as a result of the nature of the nurturance and sensitivity of their care provider – primarily their mother. As a product of the interactions and the quality of attachment, a child constructs an Internal Working Model (IWM) that represents his or her care provider, self, and the relationship between them. The IWM establishes a cognitive-affective framework that affects later psychosocial functioning.

Trust has been conceptualised in the attachment theory and research in two ways. First, trust has been viewed as the infant using the care provider as a secure base that is an integral part of the quality of attachment (Waters & Deane, 1985). Second, it has been proposed that securely as opposed to insecurely attached children develop an IWM that includes social expectations characterised by a sense of trust in others and positive thoughts regarding the intentions of other people's behaviour (Cohn, 1990). From my perspective, attachment style is a complex and multidimensional construct and it would be misguided to regard trust as synonymous with attachment.

Piagetian Theory

Piaget (1965) examined children's evaluations of lying, among other behaviours, as evidence for moral development. He proposed that young children (7 years and under) demonstrate moral realism (moral objectivity) and thus fail to take into consideration the intentions guiding communication. The young children viewed mistakes that caused harm as a lie and reprehensible – even though the consequences of the lie were unintended. By contrast, older children showed subjective morality by giving considerable weight to the intentions guiding the communication and regarded incorrect communication as a lie when intended to deceive others. Contrary to Piaget's formulations, contemporary research shows that young children do consider intentions in determining lying. The research does show, though, that children's utilisation of intentions in determining lying increase in complexity with development (Peterson, Peterson, & Seeto, 1983). Older children and adults regard lying as detrimental to trust in social relationships.

GENERALISED TRUST BELIEFS

Julian Rotter is one of the pioneers of research on trust. He is responsible (in part) for why I have embarked on the study of trust: a task that has taken my academic career. Many years ago, Rotter gave an invited talk on trust to the Department of Psychology at the University of Waterloo, which I attended. Rotter (1980) was keenly aware that trust is a fundamental issue in the dilemmas faced by modern society. Guided by Social Learning Theory, he proposed that experiences of promised negative or positive reinforcements shaped individuals' expectancies of those behaviours that generalise across social agents. As a consequence, individuals established stable generalised expectancies of the extent that the oral or written statements of other people can be relied upon. Those generalised expectancies could be acquired by direct learning from the behaviour of social agents (parents, teachers, peers, etc.) and from verbal statements regarding others made by significant people or trusted sources of communication.

THE APPROACH TO TRUST BY PAUL HARRIS AND HIS COLLEAGUES

I refer to this approach as Knowledge Acquisition Theory (KAT). Harris (2007) proposed that trust guides children's acquisition of knowledge and beliefs regarding a wide range of abstract entities/ concepts (religion, scientific evidence, history) with which they have no personal contact with. The children acquired knowledge and beliefs by depending on the information provided by social agents. Harris argued that children are not simple consumers of information but engage in an evaluation of the validity of that knowledge from a very early age.

SOCIAL CAPITAL

According to the Social Capital Approach, trust is a quality established among members of society, or social networks that bind individuals together and promote norms of reciprocal cooperation. The cooperation results in benefits to individuals themselves as well as to bystanders (Cozzolino, 2011). Social capital is regarded as a multidimensional construct that applies to relations with family and friends, neighbourhoods, citizens in society, the state, and institutions (Rostila, 2010).

ROMANTIC TRUST

There are two approaches to romantic trust: Attachment and Romantic-Faith. Regarding the Attachment Approach, Hazen and Shaver (1987) proposed that the love experienced in an adult romantic relationship is an attachment process similar to the one found in infancy. These authors conceptualised the infant patterns of attachment – secure, avoidant, and anxious-ambivalent – as forms of romantic attachment for adults. It was found that the distribution of securely attached, avoidant, and anxious-ambivalent were similar to those found in infant attachments. Based on the adults' retrospective reports of their infancy, the researchers identified continuity between the quality of attachments during infancy and the quality of romantic attachments during adulthood.

Regarding the Romantic-Faith Approach, Rempel, Holmes, and Zanna (1985) identified three types of trust in adults' romantic relationships: predictability (consistent vs inconsistent behaviour), dependability (attributed honesty and empathy), and faith (responsive and caring whatever will happen in the future). According to research by Rempel et al. (1985), trust progresses from predictability to dependability and then to faith as romantic relationships develop.

GAME THEORY

Games have been used to examine trust from the very beginning of research on the topic (e.g., Deutsch, 1958). In contemporary research, the game involves an exchange between two players in which cooperation and defection are assessed by the amount of money designated for a partner (Montague, King-Casas, & Cohen, 2006). During this exchange, one player (the investor, Player A) is given a certain amount of money or points (as proxies for money). The investor can keep all the money or decide to "invest" some amount with the partner (the trustee, or Player B), which is tripled in value as it is sent to the other player, who then decides what portion to return to the investor. It has been found that investors tend to make substantial initial offers to trustees so that the split is considered fair (e.g., if given $20 the investor may invest $10 with the trustee).

SOCIAL CONTACT AND EXCHANGE THEORIES

Social Contact and Exchange theories of trust are found in different disciplines: psychology, criminology, sociology, and organisational sciences. Trust is regarded as the product of exchanges of benevolent outcomes between individuals guided by practices of fairness and rules of justice (e.g., Schoorman, Mayer, & Davis, 2007).

THE BASES, DOMAINS, AND TARGET DIMENSIONS (BDT) FRAMEWORK

The BDT was advanced by my colleagues and myself (Rotenberg, 2010). The BDT Framework specifies that trust comprises three bases (reliability, emotional, honesty), three domains (cognitive/affect, behaviour-dependent, behaviour-enacting) and two target dimensions (familiarity, specificity). The three bases are: (1) reliability, comprising fulfilment of words or promises; (2) emotional, comprising refraining from causing emotional harm and by being receptive to disclosure and maintaining confidentiality of them; (3) honesty, comprising telling the truth and engaging in behaviour guided by benevolent rather than malevolent intention. The three domains are: (1) cognitive/affect, which comprises individuals' beliefs/feelings that others demonstrate the three bases of trust (e.g., trust beliefs); (2) behaviour-dependent, which comprises individuals behaviourally relying on others to act in a trusting fashion as per the three bases of trust; and (3) behaviour-enacting, which comprises individuals behaviourally engaging in the three bases of trust (e.g., trustworthiness). The bases and domains span across two target dimensions: familiarity, which ranges from highly to slightly familiar; and specificity, which ranges from specific others to general others. Finally, the BDT specifies that trust is a reciprocal process in which trusting beliefs and behaviours are matched by partners in dyads. These reciprocal exchanges result in a common social history of the partners.

SUMMARY

This chapter began by addressing the question of whether trust was a crisis or a theory of everything. The chapter included popular definitions of trust and concluded with summaries of theories and approaches to the topic of trust.

2

LYING AND TRUST
Sex, lies, and videotape

The role of lying and violations of trust in adult interpersonal relationships in contemporary society is aptly depicted in the film *Sex, Lies, and Videotape* produced in 1989 by Steven Soderbergh. In this provocative movie, Ann (played by Andie MacDowell) no longer has sex with her husband John (played by Peter Gallagher) who, unknown to her, has been having an affair with her sister Cynthia (played by Laura San Giacomo). The dynamics of the movie revolve around a visit to the household by an old friend of John's, a drifter by the name of Graham (played by James Spader). Graham has the unusual fetish of taping women describing their sexual experiences. Eventually Cynthia and Ann individually make videotapes describing their sexual experiences for Graham. Also, Graham finally confesses on videotape that he used to lie compulsively and that it destroyed his romantic relationships. Ann accidentally finds out that John is having an affair with her sister. She decides that John is untrustworthy and ends the marriage. Subsequently, Ann and Graham begin to develop a close relationship. The theme of this movie is that lies and deception permeate close adult relationships; this undermines trust and ends the relationships. The movie proposes that confidential disclosure on videotape can help people face and resolve sexual problems. Is this just movie madness or is it an accurate description of real life?

HOW OFTEN DO PEOPLE LIE?

Serota, Levine, and Boster (2010) asked a large sample of Americans to report on-line about how many lies they told to five types of persons (friends, family, business associates, acquaintances, and strangers) in the last 24 hours. The participants were asked to report lies regardless of whether they were obvious or subtle or selfish or to protect others. It was found that the participants reported that they lied on average two times a day. Also, it was found that only a few people report telling many lies: almost half of all lies were told by only 5% of the sample. Indeed, there appear to be a few prolific liars. It was found that lies were more likely told to family members or friends than to acquaintances or total strangers and the frequency of lying declined with age across adulthood. In a related study, DePaulo, Kashy, Kirkendol, Wyer, & Epstein (1996) had 77 college students and 70 people from the community complete diaries regarding lying for a week. It was found that college students told an average of two lies per day and people from the community told an average of one lie per day.

WHAT KINDS OF LIES DO PEOPLE TELL?

Survey research (Northrup, Schwartz, & Witte, 2013) showed that 33% of men and 19% of women admit to being unfaithful. The infidelity ranged from one-night stands to frequent liaisons (see Chapter 5). DePaulo, Ansfield, Kirkendol, & Boden (2004) found that affairs were the most frequent type of serious lies. People told serious lies about death and serious illnesses, as well as violence and danger, but less frequently than affairs. Those researchers found that serious lies were about forbidden acts, money or jobs, personal facts and feelings, and self-identities. According to the findings, the large majority of serious lies were designed to cover up bad behaviours and avoid punishment. These research findings suggest that the *Sex, Lies, and Videotape* film is not far from the truth about close relationships.

In an investigation of everyday lying or so-called white lies, DePaulo et al. (1996) found that individuals reported most frequently outright lied rather than engaging in exaggerated forms of lying or subtle lying (e.g., evading or omitting relevant details). People reported most often telling positive lies, which involved pretending to like something or someone more than they really did. In a related study, DePaulo and Kashy (1998) found that individuals told fewer lies per social interaction, and felt more uncomfortable lying in interactions with close persons than with others.

WHY DO PEOPLE TELL LIES?

It has been proposed that lying has an evolutionary function in various species including humans. The ability for species to deceive is regarded as essential to avoiding predators and securing nourishment (see Alcock, 2001). There is evidence that both humans and primates engage in tactical deception. This deception involves engaging in social manoeuvring, including forming coalitions and alliances, in order to achieve an objective (see Hall & Brosnan, 2017). One of the controversial points is whether the "deceptive" behaviour by other species is reflexive rather than a product of their intention to deceive; that is, whether it is a product of the comprehension of mental and emotional states.

Insight into the motivations for lying has been garnered by the diary method studies carried out by DePaulo et al. (1996). These researchers found that people are about twice as likely to tell self-centred lies that benefit themselves than lies benefitting others. People told self-centred lies in order to try to make themselves look better or feel better, protect themselves from embarrassment or disapproval, ensure that their feelings were not hurt, or gain the esteem and affection of others. Of course, people told some lies to obtain material gain or personal convenience. According to the study, people most often tell lies about their feelings rather than their achievements, their failures, and their whereabouts. When people told other-oriented lies, they often pretended to feel more positively than they really did feel, and to agree with other people when in fact they disagreed.

There is evidence that personality traits account for deception and lying. Kashy and DePaulo (1996) found that the personality disposition of Machiavellianism was associated with telling lies, primarily self-centred lies that gave the tellers an advantage over others and protected their interests. It was found that the personality characteristic of responsibility (i.e., the propensity to feel obligated to be honest and upright) was negatively associated with lying, notably self-centred lies. Finally, those with the personality disposition of Machiavellianism tended to view themselves as more successful liars than did other people.

ADOLESCENTS LIE TOO!

The prevalence of lying to parents by adolescents (high school students) and young adults (university students) was examined by Jensen, Arnett, Feldman, and Cauffman (2004). The participants were asked to rate on 5-point scales the frequency with which they had lied to their parents about six different issues (money, sexual behaviour, friends, parties, dating, and alcohol and drug use) in the last year. It was found that 82% of all young adults reported lying to their parents on at least one of six topical issues (money, alcohol/drugs, friends, dating, parties, and sex) with the mean incidence of lying ranging from 0.6 to 2.4 lies, depending on the issue. It was found that the adolescents lied more frequently than did the young adults, and males lied more frequently than did females. The adolescents reported that their primary motives for lying to parents were to preserve autonomy (e.g., the right to make their own decisions) and prosocial (to help others). Similarly, the adolescents regarded lying as more acceptable to parents than did the young adults. Also, males regarded lying as more acceptable to parents than did females. Finally, low dispositional self-restraint was associated with acceptance of lying to parents which, in turn, statistically predicted lying. The authors suggested that the decline in frequency of lying to parents from adolescence to adulthood was the result of the achievement of autonomy by adulthood, which decreased the need for deceptive behaviour.

DO CHILDREN KNOW WHAT A LIE IS?

Even young children (3 or 4 years of age) understand that lying depends on the intention to deceive – although there is a developmental growth in appreciation of intentions in defining lying (see Chapter 1). Theory of mind (TOM) research has demonstrated that even very young children (4 years of age or even younger) attain first-order false belief abilities and comprehend how people can cause others to hold a belief that given events or internal states can be falsely presented. The TOM research also shows that children regard intentionally causing false beliefs in others as morally wrong (Talwar & Lee, 2008).

DO YOUNG CHILDREN LIE?

Most parents will answer yes to this question, which would be correct. Children's willingness to lie is shown in the temptation resistance paradigm (Lewis et al., 1989). In this method, the child is told by a first experimenter not to peek at or play with a toy; the experimenter then leaves the room. Videotaping is done to see if the child violated the experimenter's instructions by peeking. Another experimenter then visits the child and asks him or her about his or her actions when the first experimenter was absent. This is done to see if the child admits to cheating. The studies using this method show that even preschool children (3 to 5 years of age) frequently hide the truth or conceal information to deceive others.

Longitudinal studies show that many children (around 65%) lie frequently or occasionally, according to mothers' reports. Only a small percentage (5%) of elementary school children are consistent liars (Gervais, Tremblay, & Desmarais-Gervais, 2000). This percentage is similar to the percentage of adults who chronically lie, according to the study by Serota, Levine, and Boster (2010). Several studies show that boys lie more frequently than do girls (see Lee, 2013).

WHY DO CHILDREN LIE?

Children lie or deceive primary because those actions lead to fewer negative consequences for themselves (see Talwar & Crossman, 2011). Nevertheless, some research shows that children do tell white lies in order to protect the feelings of others. In a study by Warneken and Orlins (2015) children from three age groups (5-year-olds, 7- to 8-year-olds, and 10- to 11-year-olds) interacted with an adult in an art task. During the sequence of interactions, an adult served as an artist and drew rather poor pictures, such as that of a house. The artist either expressed to the children that she was very sad about her lack of skill at being an artist (the Sad condition) or that she didn't really care about her lack of skill (the Neutral condition). The children's task was to decide whether the artist's drawing was good or bad. The children across ages were more likely to decide the drawing was good rather than bad when in the Sad than Neutral condition. The study showed that children tell white lies in order to protect the feelings of others,

CHILDREN LIE . . . BUT DO THEY KNOW THAT IT IS WRONG TO DO SO?

Research converges in showing that even very young children (3 or 4 years) morally condemn lying (see Lee, 2013). Research shows that adults view altruistic lies as more moral than they do selfish honesty (Levine & Schweitzer, 2014). There are, however, cultural and developmental differences in moral appraisals of lying. For example, Chinese children are more accepting of lying in order to protect others' feelings or the reputation of the group than are North American children. Furthermore, there is evidence that there are increases across childhood in children's acceptance of lying as a polite act and willingness to tell that type of lie (Xu, Bao, Fu, Talwar, & Lee, 2010).

ARE PEOPLE ABLE TO DETECT WHEN PEOPLE ARE LYING?

In practice, children and adults do not typically exceed chance levels in detecting when persons lie. There are exceptions to this observation:

federal law enforcers and clinical psychologists have been found to exceed chance in the detection of deception (see Crossman & Lewis, 2006). Children and adults often rely on erroneous cues to detect lying, such as the misguiding cues of avoidant gaze, planned as opposed to spontaneous communication, and rapid limb movements (see DePaulo, Lanier, & Davis, 1983; Rotenberg, 1991; Shiri & Bruce, 2008). In practice, liars appear to be less forthcoming, produce more disfluencies, their explanations are less compelling, and include fewer imperfections (DePaulo et al., 2003).

SUMMARY

The chapter began with a summary of the movie *Sex, Lies, and Videotape* in the pursuit of examining the prevalence, nature, and causes of lying. The chapter included a review of the research on lying during childhood, adolescence, and adulthood. The chapter culminated in describing the finding that people are poor at detecting deception and often misguided about the cues that reveal lying.

3

TRUST IS A DELICATE BALANCE

Cons or scams have been around since the beginning of mankind (e.g., the Trojan Horse). The newspapers and media are replete with stories about people who have been conned or scammed. One day I came across a newspaper story which ran in the *Mirror* about a doctor on the popular show Good Morning Britain. The doctor described "the horrific moment she realised the lover she met on dating site Plenty of Fish had conned her out of £150,000 – even targeting her mum without her knowledge" (*Mirror News*, August 1, 2016).

Even trust researchers are not immune! I am the UK representative for the International Society for the Study of Behavioral Development (ISSBD). I received an e-mail from the president of the ISSBD requesting that I assist a fellow ISSBD member from China to visit the UK in order to attend his sister's funeral. I eventually refused and contacted the ISSBD who confirmed it was indeed a scam. The organisation placed a description of the event on their web site in order to warn others in the organisation. Perhaps my academic background helped me to resist the scam – I really do not know.

In response to hearing about scams, an individual often asks herself or himself, "Am I too trusting" or "Do I trust the right amount?" These questions are probably fundamental to life itself – they are existential questions. Let me place them in the view advanced by Frank

Crane, who stated, "You may be deceived if you trust too much, but you will live in torment if you do not trust enough". Is Frank Crane correct? The simplest way to address these questions is by reference to the research addressing the consequences of trusting too much or trusting too little.

ARE THERE CONSEQUENCES OF TRUSTING TOO LITTLE?

A growing body research has shown that low trust promotes psychosocial maladjustment. My colleagues and I used measures derived from the BDT Framework to assess the extent to which individuals believe that others show reliability (e.g., keep promises), show emotional trustworthiness (e.g., keep information confidential), and honesty (e.g., tell the truth vs lying). In one series of studies my colleagues and I (Rotenberg et al., 2010; Studies 1, 2, & 3) found that low trust beliefs longitudinally predicted increases in loneliness for three age groupings: early childhood, middle childhood, and young adulthood. The relations between low trust and increases in loneliness were both direct and mediated by measures of disengagement from social relationships.

In one of the studies (Rotenberg et al., 2010; Study 4), female undergraduates were engaged in a "memory task". They had been randomly assigned to be in one of two conditions. The undergraduates in the priming trust condition were required to memorise a list of words that included terms concerned with trust (e.g., sincere). The purpose of memorising those words was to increase the accessibility of trusting thoughts. The undergraduates in the priming distrust condition were required to memorise words that included those on distrust (e.g., lying). The purpose of the memorisation of those words was to increase the accessibility of distrusting thoughts. Next, the undergraduates were asked to rate their feelings on an adjective checklist (including loneliness and shyness) and report their willingness to disclose personal information to others. They were next engaged in a brief conversation with another female undergraduate.

First, they choose a topic from a list they would talk about and after a very brief conversation they reported the rapport they and their conversation partner had achieved.

The findings from the study showed that, in comparison to the participants primed for trust, those participants primed for distrust reported greater feelings of loneliness and withdrawal (loneliness and shyness), a lesser willingness to disclose to others, a lesser willingness to disclose intimate topics to their conversation partner, and lower perceptions of achieving rapport in the conversation.

We interpreted the findings from all four studies in our paper as showing that low trust beliefs directly contribute to loneliness, because they result in feelings of being cut off from others. Also, low trust beliefs indirectly contribute to loneliness because they result in individuals' unwillingness to engage with others, low disclosure, and a lack of perceived rapport in interactions. There is other evidence for the problem of low-trusting people. Malti et al. (2013) found that low trust is related to aggression. Qualter et al. (2013) found that low trust beliefs in others predicted high loneliness, as well as depressive symptoms and poor general health, across the period of childhood and adolescence. Overall, the research findings show that trusting too little promotes various forms of maladjustment.

ARE THERE CONSEQUENCES OF TRUSTING TOO MUCH?

Julian Rotter (1980) posed the question: Are highly trusting people highly gullible? In order to address this question, Rotter reviewed his and others' research to determine whether individuals who held high generalised trust beliefs were particularly gullible and prone to betrayal. Rotter (1967) found a lack of association between undergraduates' scores on the Rotter Interpersonal Trust Scale and others' ratings of them as gullible (naive and easily fooled). Also, Rotter reviewed a number of studies showing that individuals with high interpersonal trust did indeed show greater trusting behaviour than those with low trust. The studies confirmed, though, that when individuals had reasons to distrust the communications in the social interaction then there were no appreciable differences between the high and low trusting groups. Rotter (1980) proposed that there was no appreciable relation between trust beliefs and gullibility, but was he correct?

Unfortunately, Rotter (1980) did not consider the full range of trust beliefs, from very low to very high. Are gullibility and psychosocial functioning associated with trust beliefs when assessed across the full range? This type of analysis would allow us to consider whether trusting too much (as well as too little) had negative consequences for psychosocial functioning. Using that type of analysis, my colleagues and I found evidence to support Crane's observations. For example, we (Rotenberg, Boulton, & Fox, 2005) found that children with both very high and very low trust beliefs in peers were more rejected by peers, more excluded by peers, and held lower perceptions of self-perceived social acceptance, than did children with the midrange of trust beliefs. Also, the children with very high and with very low trust beliefs showed elevated levels of psychological maladjustment (loneliness, depression, and anxiety) across time in comparison to the children with the midrange of trust beliefs.

In a subsequent study we found that those relations between trust beliefs and psychosocial problems extended to children's peer interactions in the playground (Rotenberg, Qualter, Barrett, & Henzi, 2014). For example, girls with very low trust beliefs in peers and those with very high trust beliefs in peers showed greater problems in peer interactions (including indirect aggression, rejection by peers, and distress) than did girls with the midrange of trust beliefs in peers.

We interpreted the findings accordingly. First, we proposed that individuals with low (and very low) trust beliefs have psychosocial problems because they are inclined to be detached from others, feel lonely, and feel withdrawn. Second, we proposed that individuals with very high trust beliefs have psychosocial problems because they are at risk of being betrayed by others: for example, very vulnerable to violations of confidentiality of disclosure. Third, we proposed that the pattern is the result of both very low and very high trust belief groups violating the social norms of trusting. Overall, our research yields support for Crane's observation by showing that both very low trusting and very high trusting individuals show psychosocial problems.

BETRAYAL!

According to our arguments, individuals who are highly trusting are prone to psychosocial problems because they are betrayed. What do we know about betrayal? Some answers are provided in Chapter 2. A study by Jones and his colleagues (Jones, Chan, & Miller, 1991) showed that women reported being betrayed and betraying most commonly by extramarital affairs. Lies were the next most common form of betrayal. For men, extramarital affairs (see Chapter 5) and betraying of a confidence were equally likely to be forms of betrayal. The vast majority of people (90% of them) said that their relationships were worse off as a result of being betrayed but a substantial number (50% of them) said that their relationships were the same or even improved when they betrayed others. When betrayed, people feel that their relationship plummets into despair. Interestingly, when people were asked about betraying others, people reported that relationships remain the same or improve. There is a self-serving basis in the perceived consequences of betraying others.

In addition, Jones and his colleagues examined betrayal in normal and institutionalised children. They found that across both groups of children, betrayals fell into three categories: teasing, telling lies or making false accusations, and gossiping and betraying confidences. As expected, institutionalised boys often reported various criminal activities as betrayal but they also cited being abandoned, rejected, and ignored by their parents as betrayals. Other betrayals included breaking promises to stop drug taking and stop seeing undesirable friends, and school failure. Overall, the institutionalised boys had more serious betrayals than the normal children.

Those authors also constructed a standardised measure, called the Interpersonal Betrayal Scale (IBS), which assessed individual differences in engaging in acts of betrayal (e.g., making a promise with no intention of keeping it). The researchers found that betrayals on the IBS for adults were (a) greater for those divorced than not divorced and (b) associated with self-endorsed characteristics of sulky, envious, cynical, and doubting paranoid, passive aggressive, and (inversely) tolerant. The researchers found that betrayals on the IBS for children were associated with reports of relationships involving jealousy, disagreement, and regret. According to the study, adults and children are vulnerable to being betrayed. These researchers did not examine, though whether being too trusting was associated with betrayal as proposed.

DO I TRUST THE "RIGHT" AMOUNT AND CAN I AVOID BEING CONNED OR BETRAYED?

Unfortunately, there are no simple means by which to determine whether someone trusts the "right" amount. Sadly, there is no shield that will prevent individuals from being betrayed when they trust – perhaps too much. To begin with, the findings are statistical outcomes: they cannot provide an answer for a given individual. Even if it were possible to determine if person was too low or too high in trust, he or she is not doomed to social failure. The findings reveal *general* proclivities shown by persons with very low and very high trust to demonstrate psychosocial problems. One other issue concerns the ability of individuals to detect when others are deceiving. As described in Chapter 2, people are poor at detecting deception – not better than chance. Normally, people are unlikely to detect a scam.

One type of resolution is provided by the BDT Framework, which posits that trust in a dyad is guided by reciprocity. According to the principle, trusting beliefs and behaviour tend to become matched over the course of dyadic interactions and establish a common psychosocial history for the persons involved. In that context, the "right" level of trust depends on the history of the exchanges of trust beliefs and behaviour between an individual and the other person in a dyadic relationship. The right level of trust for an individual regarding a given relationship is best based on the history of exchanges of trust beliefs and behaviour between him/her and the other person.

SUMMARY

This chapter addressed the delicate balance of trust representing the issue of trusting too much or too little. The reviewed research showed that both extremes of trusting are associated with psychosocial problems. The chapter culminated in the discussion of betrayal and one strategy for dealing with that problem in a given social relationship.

4

DEVELOPING TRUST

Parents can get it right!

Central to various theories in developmental psychology is the principle that parents and other social agents contribute to the development of trust during childhood. According to Attachment Theory (see Chapter 1), parental nurturance and sensitivity promote the security of attachment and children's formation of Internal Working Models of attachment; these promote their trust in others. According to KAT (see Chapter 1), children's trust in others, notably their parents, is essential to their acquisition of knowledge of the physical world and religious beliefs. According to the BDT Framework (see Chapter 1), children's trust beliefs and trust behaviour (dependence and enacting) are the product of exchanges between them and parents (and other social agents). A linked social history between children and their parents is produced by reciprocated trust beliefs and trust behaviours (which are associated) during the course of social interaction.

Despite the formulations, there is surprisingly little research that has examined precisely how and if parents affect their children's trust. There are multiple questions that are viable to pose, such as whether parents affect their children's trust in them (the parents), whether parents' trust (or related behaviour) affects their children's trust in others, and whether children's trust in their parents affects the children's social development. The purpose of this chapter is to review the relevant research regarding these questions.

DO PARENTS AFFECT THEIR CHILDREN'S TRUST IN THEM?

According to Attachment Theory, securely, as opposed to insecurely, attached children develop an Internal Working Model (IWM) that is characterised by a sense of trust in others and by positive thoughts regarding the intentions of other people's behaviours. Thus they attain social competence. Attachment Theory prescribes that parental nurturance and sensitivity promote security of attachment in the offspring. Measures of IWM include items designed to assess children's trust in their parents (e.g., easy to trust their mother; see Kerns, Klepac, & Cole, 1996). There is a substantial amount of research supporting the principle that parental nurturance and sensitivity affect security of attachment and IWM. Consequently, it seems reasonable to suggest that those forms of parenting behaviours promote children's trust in their parents. This is an inference, though, because the items assessing children's trust in their parents are embedded in IWM measures.

DOES PARENTS' TRUST AFFECT THEIR CHILDREN'S TRUST IN OTHERS?

As an answer to this question, I have examined the relation between parents' trust in others and their elementary school-age children's trust in others (Rotenberg, 1995). It was found that mothers' trust beliefs in others were correlated with their children's trust beliefs in teachers. Also, we found that fathers' trusting behaviour during a competitive vs cooperative game (i.e., a version of the Prisoner's Dilemma game) was correlated with their children's trusting behaviour in the same game with a stranger. I have interpreted these findings as suggesting that mothers' verbalisations of trust regarding others affected their children's trust beliefs in others; and fathers' trusting behaviour in playful interactions affected their children's trusting behaviour in similar interactions with unfamiliar others.

WHAT CAUSES PARENTS TO TRUST THEIR CHILDREN?

Kerr, Stattin, and Trost (1999) asked adolescents to rate their parents' trust in them (e.g., parents trust them not to hang out with bad people) and asked parents to rate their trust in their adolescents on corresponding items. The researchers found that parents' trust in their adolescents both reported by the parents and the adolescents was negatively associated with delinquency and positively associated with the adolescents' spontaneous disclosure of information to the parent. The researchers proposed that adolescents' spontaneous disclosure of thoughts, feelings, and activities to parents is a primary cause of parents' trust in the adolescent. Also, it was found that parental reports of their trust in their adolescents were associated with positive family functioning as reported by parents and adolescents.

DOES CHILDREN'S TRUST IN THEIR PARENTS AFFECT THE CHILDREN'S TRUST IN OTHERS?

As a partial answer to this question, we (Rotenberg, Bharathi, Davies, & Finch, 2013) found that elementary-school children's beliefs that their parents kept promises were associated with the extent to which the children depended on peers to keep promises; and kept promises they made to peers. These findings are consistent with the notion that children's trust beliefs in parents provide the basis for the children's trust beliefs in, and trusting behaviour towards, their peers. In another study, my colleagues and I found that the children's trust beliefs in their mothers and fathers were associated with helping peers (Rotenberg et al., 2005). Children who held high beliefs in their parents were more likely to help their peers than were children who held low trust beliefs in their parents.

Researchers have found small to modest size relations between the quality of children's attachment (secure vs insecure) and their later social competence (see Schneider, Atkinson, & Tardif, 2001). The findings may be taken to imply that children's trust in their parents, as indexed by attachment, promotes their trust in peers as indexed by social competence.

DO OTHER SOCIAL AGENTS SUCH AS SCHOOLS OR NEIGHBOURHOODS AFFECT CHILDREN'S TRUST?

The role of the school in adolescents' trust is described in the study Flanagan and Stout (2010). In this study, adolescents were administered measures of social trust (e.g., most people can be trusted), interpersonal trust (e.g., my friends keep my secrets) and school solidarity (e.g., students care about each other). Also, the adolescents reported the extent to which teachers promoted mutual respect among students and encouraged the expression of opinions. The findings represent a mixture of cross-sectional and longitudinal findings. Social trust was concurrently associated with interpersonal trust, school solidarity, and democratic climate of the school. It was found that school solidarity longitudinally predicted increases in social trust. The findings yield support for the conclusions that the qualities of the adolescents' school, in the form of solidarity and democratic climate, promote the adolescents' generalised trust in others. In a related study, Bryk and Schneider (2002) found that children's trust in the schools (broadly conceived) plays a substantive role in their social and academic adjustment.

The potential effects of neighbourhoods on trust have been shown in various studies. My colleagues and I found that parent-rated trustworthiness of the neighborhood longitudinally predicted children's reliability (promise-keeping) trust beliefs in others, and trustworthiness (keeping promises) (Rotenberg, Betts, Eisner, & Ribeaud, 2012). It was found that when children live in a trustworthy rather than untrustworthy neighborhood then they are inclined to develop trusting beliefs and trustworthiness.

ARE THERE EFFECTS OF DIVORCE ON CHILDREN'S TRUST?

One of the most disruptive experiences for children is when their parents are divorced or separated. There is a body of research supporting the conclusion that children from families with divorce show greater psychosocial maladjustment than do children from "intact" families (see Reifman, Villa, Amans, Rethinam, & Telesca, 2001). Researchers have found that, compared to children of intact families, children from families with divorce demonstrate lower generalised trust beliefs in parents (Sun & Li, 2002) and lower trust beliefs in their future spouse when they are adults (Franklin, Janoff-Bulman, & Roberts, 1990). Qualitative studies (Baker, 2005) show that children report experiencing anguish, lack of trust, and alienation when their parents get divorced.

HOW SHOULD PARENTS PROMOTE THEIR CHILD'S TRUST (ESPECIALLY IN PARENTS)?

Before addressing this question, it should be highlighted that encouraging children to adopt excessively high trust beliefs in others is not desirable because such beliefs appear to undermine their psychosocial adjustment. Nevertheless, the BDT Framework suggests that parents should promote children's basic trust in them (the parents) in order to establish a trusting parent-child relationship. According to the BDT Framework, parents can do so by fulfilling promises they have made to their child, being receptive to their child's disclosure, and demonstrating honesty in interactions with their child. However, the financial and interpersonal stresses of contemporary times do make it difficult for parents to consistently demonstrate those behaviours in their interactions with their children. Perhaps the most challenging task, though, is for parents to ensure a trusting parent-child relationship is maintained over the course of marital disharmony and a divorce. These transitions have the potential to erode children's trust in parents and, when the children are adults, trust in their marital partners.

The question also pertains to what parenting behaviours promote children's trustworthiness – including trustworthiness towards parents. Several lines of research show that parents' use of punitive discipline styles (Rotenberg et al., 2012) is counterproductive and serves to undermine rather than promote trustworthiness in children. These findings are not intended to mean that parents should not set high moral standards for their children (i.e., condemn lying) but that reliance on physical punishment is not a way to achieve desirable outcomes such as trustworthiness.

The aforementioned point is underscored by findings from a study by Hays and Carver (2014). These researchers used the temptation to resistance paradigm described in Chapter 2 with 3- and 7-year-old children. As noted in Chapter 2, children are asked by an experimenter not to peek at an attractive toy; the experimenter then leaves the room. When alone, the majority of young children peek. Another experimenter subsequently asks the child whether or not he or she peeked, which provides evidence regarding his or her willingness to lie. In Hays and Carver's version of this paradigm (2014), the children were exposed to an experimenter who had lied (i.e., by incorrectly stating there were candies in a bowl) or did not tell that lie before the attractive toy procedure. It was found that school-age children (5- to 7-year-olds) were more likely to peek at the toy and lie after peeking when they had been initially exposed to the experimenter who had lied than one who had not lied. These differences were not found in preschool children (under 5 years of age). The findings suggest that adults who lie serve as a dishonest model for school-age children and thus promote untrustworthiness in them. The findings suggest that one way to help ensure your child is trustworthy is not to lie – particularly to your child – aside from Santa Claus and other social conventions.

SUMMARY

The chapter reviewed the developmental theories and related research to suggest that sensitive and nurturing parenting promotes children's trust in parents, maternal verbalisations of trust and paternal trusting behaviour promote children's trust beliefs/behaviour towards others, and adolescents' disclosure promotes parents' trust in them. The chapter included research suggesting that divorce is detrimental to specific forms of trust beliefs in the offspring. Finally, the chapter culminated in suggestions for how parents could foster children's trust in them (the parents) by not engaging in punitive parenting and lying to their children.

5

TRUST IN ROMANTIC RELATIONSHIPS

How many shades is your romantic trust?

The novel *Fifty Shades of Grey* is quite a phenomenon. As most adults know by now, it is an erotic romance novel by E. L. James and is the first book in a trilogy. The novel traces the increasingly sexually intimate relationship between a college graduate (Anastasia Steele) and a young business magnate (Christian Grey). The book depicts highly erotic behaviour composed of bondage/discipline, dominance/ submission, and sadism/masochism (BDSM). *Fifty Shades of Grey* has topped best-seller lists around the world and has sold over 90 million copies in 52 languages.

The sex in *Fifty Shades of Grey* is extremely graphic, but what may not be as vivid is the notion that trust between partners is crucial to BDSM. The submissive or bottom (i.e., the person who receives pain in BDSM) must trust the dominant or top (i.e., the person who provides the pain in the BDSM) to exercise restraint over his or her aggressive behaviour. Tops must exercise restraint in response to bottoms' subtle nonverbal cues, often during the height of passion. Certainly, BDSM is a very distinct form of sexual behaviour but it may be viewed as a rather *stark* metaphor for other sexual and romantic relationships. It comprises a relationship in which a partner is highly vulnerable to another person as part of highly interdependent interaction intended to achieve physical intimacy and emotional closeness. Also, the interactions are guided by complex and subtle forms of verbal and nonverbal communications. At the very least, this form of sex depends on trust between sexual partners – as do all voluntary forms of sex.

People strongly believe that the success of romantic relationships depends on each partner being trustworthy and establishing a trusting relationship (Fletcher, Simpson, Thomas, & Giles, 1999). The purpose of this chapter is to address whether trust is essential to human sexuality and romantic relationships and, if so, what role it plays. It should become apparent during in the coverage of the material that there are many *shades* of trust in romantic relationships, as revealed by research on the topic.

DOES THE QUALITY OF INFANT ATTACHMENT PLAY A ROLE IN ADULTS' ROMANTIC RELATIONSHIPS?

The quality of attachment during infancy is believed to provide the social-cognitive basis for the romantic attachment styles during adulthood. Although this proposition is controversial, the quality of adults' romantic attachment styles appears to have consequences for their romantic relationships. According to attachment classifications, a person with a secure attachment romantic style is inclined to endorse a willingness to become close and trust others whereas a person with an anxious (insecure) attachment romantic style tend to both approach and avoid close relationships. Finally, a person with an avoidant (insecure) romantic attachment style tends to avoid close relationships and mistrust romantic partners.

Studies show that individuals with a secure romantic style have the most enduring romantic relationships whereas adults with an anxious romantic attachment style have the shortest romantic relationships (Feeney & Noller, 1990; Kirkpatrick & Davis, 1994). Kirkpatrick and Davis (1994) found, though, that there were stable couple relationships in which women had an anxious attachment style and men had an avoidant romantic attachment style. According to the researchers, those couples had stable relationships because they conformed to conventional sex roles (i.e., anxious feminine women and detached masculine men).

Trust is regarded as a crucial component of the quality of attachment of romantic relationships. Persons who have a secure romantic attachment style are inclined to trust their romantic partners (e.g., Mikulincer, 1998); be trusted by their romantic partners (Collins & Read, 1990); maintain trust over the course of romantic relationships (Keelan, Dion, & Dion, 1994); and cope positively with violations of trust, such as talking about those violations with a romantic partner (Mikulincer, 1998). Regarding human sexuality, Birnie-Porter and Hunt (2015) found that having an avoidant romantic attachment style was negatively associated with sexual satisfaction in exclusive dating, engaged, and married persons.

ARE THERE OTHER MODELS OF TRUST IN ROMANTIC RELATIONSHIPS?

The Faith-Romantic Approach to trust in romantic relationships has been advanced by Rempel and colleagues (e.g., see Chapter 1). The Faith-Romantic Approach posits that trust in romantic relationships is composed of the following: (1) predictability which comprises expectations of stable dispositions (honesty and caring) from past interaction; (2) dependability which comprises the willingness to put oneself at risk by intimate disclosure and reliance on another's promises, and (3) faith, which comprises feelings of confidence and security in the caring responses of the partner and the strength of the relationship. The research shows that those forms of trust emerge in that order as romantic relationships develop. It also was found that romantic partners' endorsement of Dependability and Faith trust in their romantic relationships were associated with their love and reports that their partners had intrinsic motives in the relationship (e.g., motives to ensure mutual satisfaction, and empathic concern). These researchers found that romantic partners who are high in romantic trust were inclined to make consistently positive statements about the causal role of their romantic partners in the relationship (Rempel, Ross, & Holmes, 2001).

REALLY, IT TAKES TWO TO TANGO!

Researchers have emphasised that trust between romantic partners is a dyadic process. Murray and Holmes (2009) proposed a model of mutual responsiveness in romantic relationships which involves discerning the extent to which the other is selfish and thus whether he or she would be accepting or rejecting of a partner's needs. Those perceptions, in turn, affect the partner's appraisal of risk (and trust) and his or her motivation to be connected rather than self-protective in the relationship. The model outlines the following relations. When conflict of interest arises (i.e., the partners' goals are conflicting), then perceptions of trust in the romantic relationship are affected by both the partners' mutual responsiveness to the goals and interdependence of each other, and each partner's predisposition to show (chronic) trust in the romantic relationship.

In a test of the mutual responsiveness model Shallcross and Simpson (2012) had heterosexual couples complete the Faith-Romantic Trust scale as a measure of their chronic trust. The couples were engaged in discussions in which each partner chose a goal that would require his or her partner to make a personal sacrifice or concession of some sort (e.g., making an expensive purchase). Each partner discussed that goal with his or her partner. After the discussions, the participants completed a measure of current trust (i.e., trust in the partner right now). In the study, the "asker" was the partner who posed the request and "responder" was the partner who received it. In support of the mutual responsiveness model, it was found that romantic partners (both asker and responder) with high chronic romantic trust were more likely to collaborate with, and accommodate to, the requests and goals of their romantic partner during the discussions than were partners with low chronic romantic trust. Also, it was found that that collaborative/accommodative strategy promoted the partners' perception of current trust in the romantic relationship.

ARE PERSONS TRUSTWORTHY IN ROMANTIC RELATIONSHIPS?

There are reasons to be concerned about the trustworthiness of romantic partners. *The Normal Bar* book by Northrup, Schwartz, and Witte (2013) is reviewed in Chapter 5. It showed that 33% of men and 19% of women admitted to being unfaithful; this behaviour ranged from one-night stands to frequent liaisons. Similarly, Mark, Janssen, and Milhausen (2011) found that 23.2% of men and 19.2% of women reported that they cheated during their romantic relationship. These researchers found that infidelity was associated with experiencing unhappiness in the relationship and low compatibility with partner and (for men only) sexual dissatisfaction with partner.

ARE PEOPLES' REACTIONS TO BETRAYAL INNATE?

One answer to this question is provided by the Evolutionary Theory on sexual infidelity. According to this theory, infidelities are violations of trust that pose gender-linked threats to the propagation and survival of the species. For men, infidelity is primarily a violation of the exclusivity of sexual relations (i.e., a violation of sexual exclusivity) because infidelities create uncertainty about paternity and the males' genetic link to the offspring. For women, infidelity is primarily a violation of emotional commitment (i.e., emotional infidelity) because that threatens the extent to which they believe that the male will provide the resources necessary for them and their offspring (see Buss, Larsen, Westen, & Semmelroth, 1992). In support of the evolutionary perspective, Shackelford, Buss, and Bennett (2002) found that men found it more difficult than women to forgive a romantic partner for sexual than emotional infidelity. By contrast, women were more likely than men to end a current romantic relationship because of a partner's emotional than sexual infidelity. According to the evolutionary perspective, reactions to sexual betrayal are innate and linked to gender.

WHAT CAN PEOPLE DO IN RESPONSE TO BETRAYAL AND MARITAL STRESS?

The rates of reported infidelity are not very comforting for people who want a long-term monogamous romantic relationship. Also, in contemporary times, the stresses and strains of romantic relationships are considerable and undermine individuals' commitment to their partners, confidence in their partner's motives, and ultimately trust in their romantic partners. What are romantic partners supposed to do? First of all, many relationships and marriages survive infidelity (see Northrup, Schwartz, & Witte, 2013) and thus it does not necessarily spell the end of a romantic relationship.

The study by Hannon, Rusbult, Finkel, and Kamashiro (2010) provides an insight into how relationships and marriages can be maintained after betrayal. Hannon et al. (2010) point out that there is prevailing retribution principle that serves as an impediment to the resolution of betrayal (i.e., people want to fight fire with fire). This should be avoided. According to the research, a positive resolution of betrayal is promoted by the following series of interlinked events: (1) the perpetrator of the betrayal is willing to make amends, (2) he or she provides a sincere apology for the violation of trust, (3) the victim of the betrayal is willing to forgive the violation of trust and (4) the romantic couple is willing to work towards placing the past behind them. This process is far from simple (see Hannon et al., 2010) and it is advisable to draw upon reputable marriage counselling. Regarding the strains of married life, it would be useful to adopt the mutual responsiveness model of trust in romantic relationships outlined by Murray and Holmes (2009).

WHAT ABOUT DETECTING BETRAYAL AND DECEPTION?

Adults are not very good at detecting deception from another's communication and their accuracy in doing so rarely exceeds chance (see Chapter 3). In response to potential betrayal, adults might resort to heightened surveillance of a partner's activities – in order to catch him or her in the act. The practical value of this strategy remains to be seen. Nevertheless, from a psychological perspective, surveillance undermines trust in a romantic relationship because it signals a partner's distrust in the other (see Marshall, Bejanyan, Di Castro, & Lee, 2013).

SUMMARY

The chapter began with the book *Fifty Shades of Grey* as a stark metaphor of the role of trust in romantic relationships. The chapter reviewed the research findings regarding the Attachment Theory and Faith-Romantic Approach to romantic relationships and compared the two. Finally, the chapter drew upon Evolutionary Theory as one account of the origins of trust in romantic relationships. It culminated in recommendations for how people could deal with betrayal in romantic relationships.

6

TRUST AND HEALTH

The road to wellness?

The experience of entering an operating theatre highlights the extent to which trust plays a role in medical treatment. Here you are – helpless in the hands of physicians and technology. Humans are increasingly under the care of medical professionals because of advances in medical science and as a result live longer. As in many facets of peoples' lives (see Chapter 1) though, controversies regarding trust in health professionals has emerged in contemporary society.

READ ALL ABOUT IT!

A scientific magazine headline has declared that "America's Trust in Doctors Is Failing" (Harding, 2014, n.p.). The magazine headline was based, in large part, on the paper the by Blendon, Benson, Joachim and Hero (2014). These authors reviewed historical polling data on the public's trust in US physicians and medical leaders from 1966 through 2014. The authors also considered the findings from a 29-country survey conducted from March 2011 through April 2013 as part of the International Social Survey Programme (ISSP). According to their report, the public's trust in the leaders of the US medical profession declined sharply over the past half century, with around 75% of Americans in 1966 saying that they had great confidence in the leaders of the medical profession but only 34% saying so in 2012. According to the paper, public confidence in the US health care system was currently low and only 23% expressed a great deal or quite a lot of confidence in the system. Nevertheless, the report stated the public's current trust in physicians' integrity was high, with 69% of the public rating the honesty and ethical standards of physicians as a group as "very high" or "high". In that vein, around 60% of US adults agreed in the surveys that currently, "All things considered, doctors in [your country] can be trusted" (p. 1570), although adults in some other countries agreed more with the statement. Adults in the US were very satisfied with the quality of the health care they received and ranked third of the countries in patient satisfaction. The authors proposed that the mixed pattern of findings regarding trust was due, in part, to the lack of a universal health care system in the United States.

Is America's trust in doctors failing as the above magazine title states? In my view, no! It is important to highlight, here, the problems with believing headlines. In order to get a more accurate view it is important to read the primary sources – read them very carefully. Nevertheless, the magazine article and primary source attests to the following two problems.

First, they demonstrate the confusion regarding what is a proper measure of trust in physicians/doctors. The magazine article (Harding, 2014) and the publication by Blendon et al. (2014) include an array of different terms such as "trust", "confidence", and "integrity". Although we have an intuitive understanding of these, what did they mean to the respondents and do they assess the same thing? The answer from my perspective is that their meaning is uncertain and the terms are not synonymous. Certainly patient satisfaction is separate from trust in physicians.

Second, the papers highlight the misguided strategy of confusing trust in physicians with trust in the medical system and trust in leaders in the field of medicine. Medical treatment is a multilevel construct with complex links between the leaders in the field of medicine; medical systems (e.g., socialised vs non-socialised); hospitals; treatment centres; consultants, physicians, and nurses in treatment centres; and personal physicians (see Pilgrim, Tomasini, & Vassilev, 2010). The role of trust in medical treatment is indeed complex! This chapter will focus on trust in physicians/doctors and nurses because of its prevalence in psychological research, although there is a broader domain of medical trust (e.g., leaders, systems, etc.) that is important in its own right.

DOES BEING TRUST IN GENERALISED OTHERS INCREASE OUR HEALTH?

Research has shown that the individuals who hold low generalised trust in others (see Generalised Trust Beliefs in Chapter 1) tend have shorter lives. In the study by Barefoot et al. (1998) 100 adults (44 to 80 years of age) were administered measures of generalised trust beliefs (Rotter's GTB scale), psychological well-being, life satisfaction, and functional health (self-rated health and daily activities). Mortality was assessed 14 years later. The researchers found that low generalised trust beliefs were associated with poor psychological adjustment (notably negative emotions); poor functional health, both concurrently and prospectively; and earlier mortality, which tended to be evident even when functional health was statistically controlled. The authors suggested that low generalised trust beliefs were linked to poor health/lower mortality because those relations were the results of such factors as lack of social support, cynicism, reductions in the body's immunity to illness, and unwillingness to seek out needed medical treatment. Nummela, Raivio, and Uutela (2012) have found similar relations in Southern Finland, but only for men.

DOES ADULTS' TRUST IN HEALTH PROFESSIONALS PROMOTE HEALTH?

A number of studies show that adults' trust beliefs in physicians are associated with successful medical treatment. For example, Thom and his colleagues (Thom, Kravitz, Bell, Krupat, & Azari, 2002; Thom, Ribisl, Stewart, Luke, & The Stanford Trust Study Physicians, 1999) found that adults' scores on the Trust in Physicians Scale (TPS) were associated with self-reported continuity with physician, adherence to medication, satisfaction with physician, satisfaction with their care, the intention to follow the doctor's advice, and symptom improvement after two weeks. Similar relations between adults' trust and some health-related measures have been found in studies employing other scales to assess adults' trust beliefs in physicians (see Birkhäuer et al., 2017).

Scholars have been concerned with racial differences in medical treatment as they bear on trust. In particular, researchers have found racial disparities in the treatment of HIV (see Saha, Jacobs, Moore, & Beach, 2010). Black people are less likely to receive antiretroviral therapy (ART) than Caucasian people. Saha et al. (2010) proposed that lower trust in physicians by Black people than Caucasian people would account for their lower medical treatment of AIDS. In the study, 1,327 patients (1,104 Black) rated: (a) how much they trusted their physicians, (b) the quality of their life, (c) quality of patient-provider interaction, and (d) whether they had received ART (cross-checked with clinical records). Also, the patients' CD4 lymphocyte counts were obtained from clinical records. The researchers found that, compared to Caucasian people, Black people were less trusting in their physicians, less likely to receive ART, less likely to adhere to ART, and less likely to achieve viral suppression. Also it was found that trust in physicians was associated with adherence to ART. The findings showed that the Black people who had complete trust in their physicians were similar to Caucasian people in adhering to ART. The researchers argued that racial disparity between Black and Caucasian people in the treatment of HIV is a product, in part, of Black people's low trust in physicians and resulting lack of adherence to ART.

DOES CHILDREN'S/ADOLESCENT'S TRUST IN HEALTH PROFESSIONALS PROMOTE HEALTH?

One answer to this question is provided by the research that my colleagues and I have carried out on children's/adolescents' trust in physicians and nurses. Guided by the BDT Framework, we carried out studies on children (around 10 years of age) to develop a Children's Trust in General Physicians Scale (CTGPS; Rotenberg et al., 2008) and Children's Trust General Nurses Scale (CTGNS; Rotenberg, Woods, & Betts, 2015). The analyses confirmed that the CTGPS and CTGNS assessed the three bases of trust: reliability, emotional, and honesty. As expected, it was found that the CTGPS (notably emotional trust subscale) scores were associated with the reports of how much children trusted doctors, and the children's adherence to prescribed medical regimes. The latter finding yielded support for the principle that trust in physicians promotes adherence. It was found that the CTGNS scores were associated with children's "trust" in, but not "fear" of, nurses. Finally, it was found that the CTGNS were associated with parent's reports of the frequency with which they and their children visited medical centres. The latter finding supported the hypothesis that the more frequently the children interacted with nurses then the more they trusted nurses. Broadly, the findings support the conclusion that children's trust in health professionals (physicians and nurses) promotes physical health.

DOES A PERSON'S TRUST IN HIS OR HER MARRIAGE PARTNER PROMOTE HIS OR HER HEALTH?

An answer to this question is provided in the study by Schneider, Konijn, Righetti, and Rusbult (2011). At 26 years of age, individuals from married couples were administered the Faith-Romance Trust Scale (Rempel et al., 1985, see Chapter 5), a physical health scale (33 potential health problems), and evaluations of measures of mental health (depression and anxiety). The couples were administered these across five successive 6-month time periods. It was found that trust in a romantic partner longitudinally predicted self-reported health and the findings supported the conclusion that trust in marriage partners is a probable cause of health. Furthermore, the findings showed that that relation was mediated by mental health (low anxiety and depression), which supported the conclusion that trust caused health, in part, because it promoted mental health.

WHAT ROLE DOES TRUST PLAY IN EATING DISORDERS?

Obesity is regarded as an epidemic in the United Kingdom and the United States, as well as around the world (Hruby & Hu, 2015). Less prevalent but still a serious problem are the eating disorders of anorexia nervosa, bulimia nervosa, and binge eating disorders. Anorexia nervosa is diagnosed, in part, from a body mass index of less than 85% and severe and selective restriction of food intake. Bulimia nervosa is diagnosed, in part, as attempts to restrict food intake that are punctuated by repeated binges and self-induced vomiting. By the age of 20, 15% of women have one of these three eating disorders (Stice, Marti, & Rohde, 2013). The percentage is about half of that for men.

All types of eating disorders pose risks to mental and physical health. Obesity increases the risk of heart disease and diabetes (Yan et al., 2004) and psychological problems such as depression (Papadopoulos & Brennan, 2015). Studies show that those with anorexia nervosa, bulimia nervosa, and binge eating disorders are inclined to have psychological problems (e.g., depression, loneliness), and suicidal tendencies (Fairburn & Harrison, 2003).

My colleagues and I have examined the role of trust in eating disorders and health as part of the Social Withdrawal Syndrome (SWS). The SWS comprises a coherent pattern of low trust beliefs in others, low disclosure to others, and heightened loneliness. In one study, we found that bulimic symptoms in young adults were associated with low trust beliefs in close others (mother, father, and friends), an unwillingness to disclose personal information to them, and high loneliness (Rotenberg et al., 2013). In a re-analysis of that data using Body Mass Index (BMI), we found that obese individuals similarly showed the SWS pattern (Rotenberg, Bharathi, Davies, & Finch, 2017). In another study, my colleagues and I found that low trust beliefs in close others (mother, father, and friend) by early adolescents (11 to 12 years of age) predicted an increase in their bulimic symptoms across a 5-month period (Rotenberg & Sangha, 2015). Also, we found that that predictive relation was due, in part, to the relation between low trust beliefs and loneliness. Overall, the findings support the hypothesis that bulimia nervosa and obesity are associated with the Social Withdrawal Syndrome. Also, we proposed that because of the SWS, those with eating disorders were at risk for psychological and physical health problems, The SWS caused them to withhold information about their eating and emotional problems from health professionals which decreased the likelihood that they would be treated for their problems.

ARE THERE CONSEQUENCES OF BEING TOO TRUSTING IN THE MEDICAL PROFESSION?

It may be posed that being highly trusting in medical professionals makes an individual too passive, too gullible, and unengaged in interactions with health professionals – all of which would decrease the likelihood of proper medical treatment. This view is frequently raised by authors who advocate that medical/health education and information be provided to patients in order to empower them and increase their chances of receiving proper medical treatment (see Pilgrim, Tomasini, & Vassilev, 2010). As yet, researchers have not reported curvilinear relationships between trust beliefs in health professionals and health behaviours. One promising approach to this issue resides in the implementation of a physician-patient working alliance that entails empathy, trust, and shared decision-making in physician-patient relationships. The physician-patient working alliance has been found to be associated with patient adherence, satisfaction, and improved patient outcomes (see Fuertes, Toporovsky, Reyes, & Osborne, 2017). These findings may be interpreted as indicating that some blend of patients' trust in physicians and shared decision-making with physicians is optimally associated with health.

SUMMARY

This chapter reviews the research showing that generalised trust, trust in health professionals, and trust in romantic partners are associated with health (e.g., longevity and adherence to prescribed medical regimes). The chapter addressed the apparent racial disparities of HIV treatment and trust in physicians, as well as the relation between eating disorders and the lack of trust. The chapter culminates in describing physician-patient working alliance programs as an important blend of trust and joint decision-making in medical treatment.

7

TRUST IN THE POLICE

Do you trust the police?

Philando Castile, a 32-year-old Black man, was shot in his car by a Minnesota police officer. A live video of the shooting was posted on Facebook by Castile's girlfriend, who had been in the car at the time. Castile had told the officer that he had a licensed firearm and reached for his wallet. The gunshot wounds resulted in death. According to the video, the officer told Castile not to move. As Castile was putting his hands back up, the officer shot him in the arm four or five times. This is not an isolated incident in the US. The number of Americans killed by the police each year is substantial: there 807 to date of this chapter and most are from minority groups (see Guardian News, 2015). Public websites now document the individuals in the US who have been killed by the police (e.g., http://killedbypolice.net/). The laws have now changed and police in the US are required to report those killings quarterly (see Guardian News, 2016). Katz (2015) has proposed that police killings in the US should be prosecuted by agencies or groups independent of the existing legal system, such as a police ombudsman or a Bureau of the Investigation of Police Affairs.

Other events now show how dire some police-community relationships have become. On Thursday evening (July 7, 2016) in Belo Garden Park, Dallas, 12 police officers were shot by two snipers: 5 were killed and 7 were injured. The attack occurred after a rally protesting the deaths of two Black men at the hands of the police. In the aftermath, marches have been held in the US that protested the police killings of minorities, particularly Black men (see http://edition.cnn.com/2016/07/10/us/black-lives-matter-protests/). Trust in the police is perhaps the most controversial issue in the US in contemporary times. There is evidence that it is a growing problem around the world.

The aforementioned events throw in high relief the view that the public's trust in the police is essential to the maintenance of social order. For example, Tyler and Huo (2002) found that individuals' trust in legal authorities such as the police was associated with their compliance with authorities' decisions and laws. It has been argued that without such trust, society is at risk for lawbreaking and misconduct, and police have difficulty in carrying out their law enforcement duties (Goldsmith, 2005; Sunshine & Tyler, 2003). In that vein, being a police officer is one of the most stressful occupations in contemporary society (see Ortega, Brenner, & Leather, 2007). The job may become more stressful yet.

IS TRUST IN THE POLICE AS LOW AS IMPLIED BY THESE EVENTS?

Views of how much the public trust the police vary dramatically, particularly in the US. McNamara (2012) has insisted that trust in the police in the US is very strong. By contrast, Williams (2010) has insisted that trust in the police in the US is low – largely because of police brutality (as per the introduction to this chapter). Which is it? Before answering this question, several cautions need to be expressed. First, researchers in psychology tend not to claim that the scales have absolute values. Rather, researchers regard scales as relative measures that permit comparisons (e.g., whether trust is lower or higher). Also, one major issue is how trust is assessed. In studies on the topic of the public trust the police, people have been asked to make single judgments regarding their "trust" or "confidence" – which have uncertain meanings, Furthermore, the meanings of those terms are likely different for different individuals and for different cultures.

With those limitations in mind, here are some of the findings. A 2009–2010 British Crime Survey by the Home Office reported that only 46% of people residing in the UK have confidence in the police. Derek Prall (2014) reported the findings from a Gallup poll phone survey of approximately 1,000 adults who were sampled from generally high-income, democratic countries in the Organisation for Economic Co-operation and Development. Americans' confidence in local police fell in the middle of the group of countries, with 78% of Americans reporting they had confidence in the police. Trust (confidence) in the police is low in Latin America and that has been attributed to elevated crime rates (notably being a victim of crime), and poor political and economic performance (Corbacho, Philipp, & Ruiz-Vega, 2015; Jamison, 2011). Self-reported confidence or trust in police is very low in Russia and that has been attributed to corruption – including bribery, unfair treatment, and abuse of power (Semukhina & Reynolds, 2014).

An analysis of the 2004 European Social Survey (ESS) was carried out by Kääriäinen (2007), which required individuals to rate how much they personally trusted the police. The data analysis of samples from 16 countries showed that the top four countries for trust in the police were Nordic countries: Finland, Denmark, Norway, and Sweden. The next ranked countries in trust in the police were Central and West European countries such as Germany, Luxembourg, Austria, and the UK The countries with the lowest trust in the police were mainly in post-socialist countries such as the Czech Republic, Poland, and Slovenia. The research showed that trust in the police was statistically associated with (in order from highest to lowest) perceived corruption, welfare expenditure of GNP, and how safe people felt walking alone in their local areas after dark. Interestingly, trust in the police was not appreciably associated with being a victim of burglary. Finally, it was found that perceived corruption primarily accounted (in statistical terms) for the differences between the countries in their trust in the police.

TO WHAT EXTENT ARE THE POLICE CORRUPT?

One insight into this issue is provided by Porter and Warrender (2009) who coded 50 cases of records of criminality by the police. The analyses yielded three types of deviant behaviour in the police:

(a) police crime, (b) noble cause misconduct, and (c) corruption. The researchers reported that Police Crime usually involved constables committing proactive single criminal offences alone. Personal gain was the most frequent motive. As the authors noted, objective data on corruption is difficult to obtain because of limited access to that information by legal authorities and by officers' unwillingness to report the deviance of fellow officers. Other researchers have identified what has been called the "code of silence", which involves police officers' unwillingness to report criminal activities by other fellow officers (Ivković, Peacock, & Haberfeld, 2016).

WHAT ABOUT JUSTICE AND TRUST?

Tyler and his colleagues (e.g., Tyler, 2015; Sunshine & Tyler, 2003) have examined trust in police in relation to procedural justice and legitimacy. "Procedural justice" refers to the extent to which police are believed to make decisions and exercise their authority in a fair fashion. "Legitimacy" corresponds to confidence in authority of the police. According to this approach, people accept the legal decisions and actions of the police (and courts) when those decisions and acts are viewed as fair as well as legitimate. For example, Tyler and his colleagues (Tyler, 2001) found that perceptions of trust in the police (and courts) by majority and minority Americans are associated with their perceptions of procedural justice, which included being treated fairly by the police.

Other studies have examined the relations between trust and procedural justice in the police organisation. Sholihin and Pike (2010) found that senior police officers' trust in their supervisors (e.g., felt free to discuss matters with supervisor) was associated with perceptions of procedural fairness and their commitment to the police force. Furthermore, the relation between procedural fairness and commitment was found to be mediated by the police officers' trust in their supervisors. The researchers argued that the officers' trust in their superiors affected their commitment to the police force and that was responsible (in part) for the relation between perceived procedural fairness of the police force and commitment to the force.

ARE THERE RACIAL BIASES IN THE PUBLICS' TRUST IN THE POLICE?

A number of studies have shown that trust in the police in the US is associated with race. Minorities (notably Black people), show lower trust in the police than do majorities (e.g., MacDonald & Stokes, 2006; Thompson & Kahn, 2016). For example, MacDonald and Stokes (2006) used the data gathered by the Social Capital Benchmark Survey, which was a national random-digit dial telephone survey of 3,003 US residents. The participants completed a 3-point rating of their trust in their local police; the Social Capital Benchmark Survey, which included items assessing their trust and civic engagement in communities (including self-reported trust in their neighbours); and demographic measures (e.g., race, income, and age). The researchers found that self-reported trust in the police was positively associated with social capital, age, and income. Black people reported lower trust in police than did Caucasian people and race was the strongest statistical predictor of that trust, compared to the other variables. The findings lend support to the Social Capital Approach to trust (see Chapter 1). One account of the racial biases in trust in the police is advanced by Tyler (2001) as part of the procedural justice approach. His findings supported the conclusion that the observed racial differences in trust in the police are the result of Black people regarding their treatment by the police (and courts) as comparatively unfair.

ARE POLICE OFFICERS RACIALLY BIASED IN THEIR DUTIES?

The research using the shooter task yields some evidence for racial biases. For the shooter task, individuals are posed with the task of using a handgun to deal with a perpetrator of a crime. The individuals are shown images of Black people and Caucasian people (potential perpetrators) holding either a gun or a neutral object (e.g., a cell phone). The individuals are given less than one second to decide whether to shoot or not to shoot the target. A meta-analysis by Mekawi and Bresin (2015) has shown that individuals are quicker to shoot armed Black targets, slower to not shoot unarmed Black targets, and have a liberal shooting threshold for Black targets. The meta-analysis revealed that the shooting biases were found in police officers, community members, and undergraduates. According to these studies, police (as well as other people) have racial biases in the shooting of potential suspects.

Some authors have voiced concerns over the reliability of those racially biased shooter effects. Correll, Hudson, Guillermo, and Ma (2014) have failed to find those shooter biases in police officers on some measures. These researchers highlight the importance of identifying factors that reduce the likelihood that police officers demonstrate the shooter bias and helping police officers to adopt strategies for controlling their attention to irrelevant cues in their policing duties.

Finally, data from major cities such as New York indicate that Black people are disproportionately the victims of police misconduct (see Katz, 2015). It is difficult to draw simple and definitive conclusions regarding racial biases in policing. It is important to be mindful of the moral and social complexity of the situation. In particular, the observed relations and patterns are enmeshed in the dynamics of law enforcer and potential perpetrator of the crime (they are reciprocal) and the emotional rhetoric regarding the relationships between the minority citizens and the police force.

WHAT ARE THE CONSEQUENCES OF POLICE OFFICERS' OWN TRUST IN THE POLICE?

The BDT Framework is a useful way of assessing trust beliefs in the police because it permits explicit judgments of trustworthiness of police as part of their duties. Those include promising to provide protection to citizens (reliability-based trust), maintaining confidentiality of witness's personal information (emotional-based trust), reporting criminal events accurately (honesty-based trust). My colleagues and I (Rotenberg, Harrison, & Reeves, 2016) have developed a Trust Beliefs in Police scale guided by the BDT Framework. Individuals are presented brief vignettes that depict the potential for police officers to demonstrate reliability, emotional trustworthiness, and honesty behaviours as part of their normal duties. Individuals judge the likelihood (expectation) that the police officers will engage in those behaviours. Because of the specificity and concreteness of the items on these scales, they are less susceptible to the problems of generality, abstractness, and social desirability that confront the use of other measures of trust in the police.

My colleagues and I (Rotenberg et al., 2016) used the Trust Beliefs in Police (TBP) scale to investigate police officers' trust beliefs in the police. In the study, police officers completed the TBP scale from their perspective as a measure of their personal trust beliefs in the police. They also completed the TBP scale from the perspective of the community as a measure of public-ascribed trust beliefs in the police. The TBP scales yielded measures of three types of trust beliefs (in accordance with the BDT Framework): reliability, emotional, and honesty. The police officers also were administered standardised measures of their psychological well-being and stress in the workplace. It was found that the police officers held higher personal honesty-based and emotional-based trust beliefs in the police than they ascribed to the public. Specifically, compared to the police officers' personal beliefs, the police officers reported that the community held lower beliefs that the police would refrain from emotional harm and demonstrate honesty. Also, police officers' reliability-based personal trust beliefs in the police were positively associated with their psychological well-being and negatively associated with their stress in the workplace. Finally, police officers' emotion-based publicly-ascribed trust beliefs in the police were positively associated with their psychological well-being and tended to be negatively associated with their stress in the workplace. The findings confirmed that police officers' trust beliefs in the police are associated with their psychological well-being and low stress in the workplace.

SUMMARY

The chapter reviews the controversial issues regarding police shootings and the survey research regarding whether trust in the police is high or low. The chapter reviews the research on corruption in the police, racial bias by the police, procedural justice and trust, and racial biases in people's trust of the police. The chapter culminates in research showing that police officers' trust in the police force is associated with their psychological well-being and low stress.

8

TRUST IN THE WORKPLACE

The unseen and seen facets of trust

One unusual insight into the role that trust plays within organisations is provided by the pantomime. Panto (as it is called) is a type of musical comedy stage production designed for family entertainment in the UK. Typically, there is a fight between good and evil with the heroes winning the day. One hero is a dame who is a man dressed up as a woman. At one point in the panto, the heroes stand or sit in a line facing the audience. The villain runs behind them and then off the stage into the wings. The audience, which normally includes children, say "He's behind you" to which one of the heroes says, "No, he is not". The villain does that again. The hero looks around and says he or she can't see him and where is he? – after which the villain returns. This sequence is repeated several times. This scenario is central to the comedy of the panto and represents interplay between the audience and the heroes in helping them deal with an unseen threat and evil. This rather odd scenario pertains to trust within organisations simply because some behaviour within an organisation is an unseen, unknown act of deception. Such acts may well have a profound effect on an employee's trust and well-being. Other people in the workplace may observe those acts of deception (similar to the audience in the panto) but unlike the panto they may or not be willing to share those observations with the employee.

Before progressing on this topic it should be highlighted that the bulk of theory and research on trust in organisations is guided by the principle that an employee's trust within the workplace contributes to his or her psychological adjustment, his or her performance in the workplace, as well as the success of the employer and organisation (e.g., Cook & Wall, 1980; Paillé, Bourdeau, & Galois, 2010). This is one of the guiding premises of investigations of the topic.

THE UNSEEN HAND!

The role of the unseen hand in trust in the workplace is shown by a study by Baron and Neuman (1996). The research was guided by the principle that individuals are inclined to engage in those aggressive behaviours that are effective in harming the victim whilst incurring as little danger to them (the individuals) as possible. It was expected that much aggression in the workplace would be covert, disguising the identity of the perpetrator and leaving the victim uncertain as to whether the harm experienced was intentional. It was expected then that individuals in the workplace would be inclined to engage in aggression that would be verbal (e.g., harm by words rather than deeds), passive (e. g., harming by the withholding of some action), and indirect (e.g., causing harm through other agents). By that token individuals would be less inclined to engage in aggression in the workplace that was physical (e.g., harm by deeds), active (e.g., harming by performing the behaviour), and direct (harm delivered directly to the victim).

In the study, 78 employees from public and private organisations reported the frequency with which they witnessed and personally experienced different types of aggression. Consistent with expectation, verbal aggression was more frequent than physical aggression and passive aggression was more frequent than active forms of aggression. Contrary to expectations, though, direct aggression was more frequent than indirect aggression. The pattern of findings was the same for experienced aggression and witnessed aggression. The findings support the conclusion that employees in the workplace are likely to engage in some covert aggressive behaviours insofar as they are likely to be verbal and passive. The authors speculate that direct aggression might be more worthy as an action than indirect aggression because the former causes more harm to the victim.

As further support for their hypotheses, Baron, Neuman, and Geddes (1999) found in another study that employees of business organisations reported more incidents of covert than overt aggressive behaviour in the workplace. Those aggressive behaviours were associated with the employee's perceived injustice in their relations with supervisors. Finally, it was found that employees were most likely to aggress against a co-worker or their immediate supervisor than against subordinates and the organisation.

From the perspective of the BDT Framework (see Chapter 1), it is important to notice that employees reported the following aggressive behaviours in the workplace: failing to deny false rumours about the target (verbal-passive-indirect); spreading false rumours about the target (verbal-active-indirect); belittling someone's opinions to others (verbal-active-indirect); failing to take steps that would protect the target's welfare or safety (physical-passive-indirect); and reducing others' opportunities to express themselves, such as scheduling them at the end of a session so that they don't get their turn (physical-passive-direct). According to the BDT Framework, these types of aggression are untrustworthy behaviours (violating promises, violating confidentiality, and being dishonest) which would undermine trust beliefs in the workplace. The workplace may well be a dangerous place. If the panto question was posed in the workplace, then the answer would be: "Yes, he is behind you".

VULNERABILITY TO RISK: A SEEN HAND!

Social exchange theories and related research examine observable or seen behaviours within organisations (see Chapter 1). Mayer, Davis, and Schoorman (1995) defined trust within organisations as

> The willingness of a party to be vulnerable to the actions of another party based on the expectation that the other party will

perform a particular action important to the trustor, irrespective
of the ability to monitor or control the other party.

(p. 712)

According to their conceptual model, a party's trust and trusting
action in the workplace is the result of his or her propensity to trust
(e.g., predisposition to believe others keep promises), and perceived
trustworthiness of the other party (ability, benevolence, and integrity). Perceived ability comprises perceptions of the other party's
skills, competencies, and expertise in a given domain. Perceived
benevolence comprises the extent to which the other party is believed
to be engaged in actions intended to benefit the party in question
(i.e., do him good). Finally, perceived integrity comprises the perception that the other party adheres to a set of acceptable principles
such as demonstrating credible communications and a strong sense
of justice, and manifesting words into actions. The party's trust is his
or her willingness to be vulnerable to risk in the workplace, which
is ultimately shown by engaging in the trusting action of assuming
that risk in a given business context. In a subsequent revision of this
approach, Schoorman, Mayer, and Davis (2007) proposed that trust
does involve the reciprocal willingness of two parties to be vulnerable, although not uniformly so (i.e., leader-member exchanges).

Evidence has accumulated to support the vulnerability to risk
approach to trust in the workplace. For example, Tan and Lim (2009)
tested 126 insurance agents from 14 agencies. The findings confirmed
that the three trustworthiness attributes of co-workers (ability, benevolence, and integrity) statistically predicted the employee's trust in his
or her co-workers. Also, it was found that that trust statistically predicted the employees' commitment to the organisation and performance in the workplace. This approach has received further support
from longitudinal studies. Ferrin, Bligh, and Kohles (2008) found
that there are reciprocal relationships between perceived trustworthiness and co-operation between co-workers which formed a spiral
across time.

Researchers have tested the implications of the vulnerability to risk conceptualisation for the relationships between managers and workers. In a quasi-experiment, Mayer and Davis (1999) investigated the differences between naturally occurring groups of employees from a small non-union plastics manufacturing firm in the US Midwest. The employees were administered three waves of surveys over a period of 14 months. During the period, a new appraisal system for employees was implemented. The system involved a supervisor and employee meeting to reconcile their appraisals with supervisors specifying to the worker the expected and desired behaviours and outcomes of employment (i.e., a transparent strategy). During the course of the study, some employees (participants) had been appraised under the new system and others had not. The employees reported on standardised scales their perceptions of the trustworthiness of the management (ability, benevolence, and integrity) and trust in management. Finally, the employees reported the accuracy of the supervisors' evaluation of them (perceived accuracy) and their belief that performance will lead to desired organisational outcomes such as raises and promotions (instrumentality).

In support of the vulnerability risk conceptualisation, the researchers found that there were associations between perceived trustworthiness (ability, benevolence, integrity) of managers, trust in managers, perceived accuracy and instrumentality. Furthermore, it was found that employees who had experienced the change to the new management system showed increases across time in perceived trustworthiness of managers, trust in managers, perceived accuracy and instrumentality. Those increases were not shown by employees who had not experienced the change to the new management system. The study supports the notion that the use of transparent management strategies can promote employees' confidence in the trustworthiness of their managers and trust in them, which in turn increases their confidence that promotion would be linked to good performance on the job.

JUSTICE: ANOTHER SEEN HAND!

One line of social exchange research emphasises the role that justice plays in trust within organisations. In this line of investigation, researchers have distinguished between distributive justice, representing the perceived fairness of outcomes; procedural justice, representing the process by which allocations were made; and interactional justice, representing the communication process, such as its politeness, honesty, and respect (see Cohen-Charash & Spector, 2001). The meta-analysis of 190 studies by Cohen-Charash and Spector (2001) showed that workers' trust in their organisation was substantively associated with perceived procedural justice, distributive justice, and interactional justice. Also, the meta-analysis showed that trust in supervisors was strongly associated with perceived procedural justice and distributive justice.

Researchers have applied the principle of perceived justice to trust within the police organisation (see Chapter 7). Trinkner, Tyler, and Goff (2016) found that police officers who viewed their supervisors and co-workers as procedurally fair also reported greater trust in, and feelings of obligation to obey, their supervisors. To place this in perspective, police officers who viewed their supervisors and co-workers as procedurally unfair showed elevated psychological and emotional distress, cynicism, and mistrust – towards both the world in general and the communities they served.

SUMMARY

The chapter examines the unseen and seen facets of trust in the workplace. The unseen facets of trust in the workplace were described from the studies by Baron and his colleagues and interpreted from the BDT Framework. The seen facets of trust in the workplace were addressed by the theory and research regarding social exchange and procedural justice.

9

TRUST AND POLITICS

The Emperor's not very new clothes

"The Emperor's New Clothes", a story by Hans Christian Andersen written in 1837, is about a vain Emperor who cared only about wearing and displaying clothes. In the story, two weavers produce for the Emperor what they say is the finest, best suit of clothes made from a fabric that is invisible to anyone who is unfit for his position or hopelessly stupid. The clothes are non-existent, but the Emperor wears them for fear of being thought unfit for his position or stupid. The Emperor's ministers pretend to see the new clothes for the same reason. The Emperor wears his new clothes in a procession through the town before his subjects, who go along with the pretence because they also did not want to appear unfit or stupid. During the procession, a naïve young child in the crowd blurts out that the Emperor is wearing nothing at all – which is then taken up by others in the crowd. Although the Emperor thinks the assertion is true, he continues the procession. The story has been made into a play and a movie, to the delight of many generations.

In its simplicity, the Emperor's New Clothes story depicts a leader who is deceived. The deception is perpetuated by himself, his ministers, and the people in the town for the sake of their self-esteem and public respect. The consensual deception is challenged by a young child, who is naïve to societal pressures. The story may be regarded as a metaphor for political leadership and political power in contemporary times. Political leaders collaborate with their ministers on deceptive policies that by social communications achieve a consensual acceptance by their citizens. The veracity of those communications and actions may be challenged by opposing political parties and by vigilant media – the metaphorical child. Is the Emperor's (now not so) New Clothes an accurate description of politics and government in contemporary times? It represents a *very* cynical view of no-truth politics – a political cynicism presumably shown in Australia and the US (see Leigh, 2002).

THE FALL OF DEMOCRACY?

It is often stated that a degree of political cynicism is required for political health, but a wide array of authors believe that a fundamental trust in politicians and government is required for democracy to work (see Warren, 1999, 2004). The lack of trust in government by citizens in democracies undermines their participation in the political process and adherence to government policies (see Garen & Clark, 2015). Trust in government has been viewed as social capital, which promotes people's political involvement among other forms of civic activities (see Chapter 1). The purpose of this chapter is to review psychological research, as well as other sources, regarding the factors that affect citizens' trust in politicians and government and the consequences of that trust.

Trust in politicians/government is multi-levelled. This issue can be described, in part, by the two target dimensions of the BDT Framework (see Chapter 1). This includes specificity that ranges from specific to general, and familiarity that ranges from somewhat familiar to very familiar. For example, some political scholars have concluded that citizens' trust in Congress is at an all-time low but that citizens' trust in their own congressman or congresswoman is quite strong (Fisher, van Heerde, & Tucker, 2010). Trust in leaders (e.g., a President or Prime Minister) is conventionally different from trust in individual members of the same political party and the leader's political party (see Rotenberg, 2016). Other researchers have found that people's trust in the nature of government (i.e., as a democracy) is distinct from people's trust in an existing government (e.g., Schiffman, Thelen, & Sherman, 2010). The target of trust is an important consideration.

Other researchers have proposed that there are different forms or types of trust. For example, Fisher, van Heerde, and Tucker (2010) proposed that there are three different types of trust: strategic trust, moral trust, and deliberative trust. These researchers tested their hypothesis using the data gathered from YouGov's weekly online British Omnibus survey (n = 1,753; July 2007) and the British Election Study Continual Monitoring Panel (n = 1,018; March 2009). The survey included 13 questions designed to assess each type of trust judgment, including the following: on balance, politicians deliver on their promises (strategic trust); politicians share the same goals and values as me (moral trust); and parties represent supporters, not funders (deliberative trust). The participants reported how much trust they had in parties and politicians on an 11-point scale. In support of their formulations, the researchers found that items assessing each of the different types of trust (as identified above) statistically predicted the individuals' rating of how much they trusted the government.

DOES TRUST IN GOVERNMENT AFFECT CITIZENS' BEHAVIOUR IN DEMOCRATIC COUNTRIES?

In order to address that question, Martin (2010) used data gathered from the 2007 Australian Election Study. The citizens were administered scales assessing their trust in government. The majority of the public expressed an untrusting attitude towards government, with 58% of respondents saying members of the government usually or sometimes look after themselves. By contrast, only 43% of the public agreed that government can usually or sometimes be trusted to do the right thing. Finally, only 15% of respondents expressed the most trusting attitude (i.e., that the government can usually be trusted to do the right thing). The findings were interpreted as the Australian public demonstrating political cynicism. It was found, though, that the measure of trust in politicians was positively associated with positive attitudes towards democracy, positively associated with voting when it is not compulsory, and negatively associated with voicing frustration through challenging forms of activities (e.g., engaging in protests). The findings support the contention that trust in the government contributes to democracy.

IT WAS THE BEST OF TIMES, IT WAS THE WORST OF TIMES! (MOSTLY THE LATTER)

There is evidence indicating that political trust has been declining since the mid-1960s in many democratic countries (Blind, 2007). Cheng, Bynner, Wiggins, and Schoon (2012) have proposed that that decline is a global phenomenon. Evidence for changes in political trust and the factors affecting it have been found in a study by Hetherington and Rudolph (2008). These researchers carried out a time-series analysis, from 1976–2006, on the factors that affected political trust in the US. Trust in the government was assessed by individuals' reports that "the government in Washington will do what is right". Overall, the researchers reported that trust in government declined over time. It was found, though, that political trust increased when the public viewed international issues as vital (e.g., terrorism, national security, war, and the Middle East). Furthermore, it was found that political trust decreased when the public thought that there were problems with the economy (i.e., a period of depression). The effects of economic concern were found to result in asymmetry, insofar as relatively few people regard the economy as good, even in good times. According to the authors, the positive effects of a good economy on political trust were relatively weak and thus they failed to offset the effects of bad economies, which resulted in the decline in citizens' trust in government. The findings may indicate that the US public is on the path to viewing politicians as emperors in new clothes.

DO POLITICAL SCANDALS MATTER?

It was around 50 years ago that Watergate burst upon us. The bitter political path spanned the period from the bugging of the Democratic National Committee headquarters at the Watergate hotel on May 28, 1971 to the resignation of President Richard Nixon on August 9, 1974. Hetherington and Rudolph (2008) found that government scandals (e.g., the Clinton impeachment proceedings) predicted declines in trust in government across time. The effects were not as substantial, though, as the effects of economic and international issues on trust in government. There is evidence that government scandals have negative effects on trust in government in countries other than the US. For example, qualitative research carried out by Isotalus and Almonkari (2014) indicates that political scandals had negative effects on citizens' trust in Finland.

WHAT CAUSES THE PUBLIC TO VIEW A POLITICIAN AS TRUSTWORTHY?

The trustworthiness of political candidates emerged, for example, during the 2016 US presidential race. Perceptions of the trustworthiness of politicians have been the focus of surveys and those have been the source of discussion in the media (e.g., Kolbert, 2016). It has been noted that many politicians lacked trustworthiness during the campaign regarding whether the UK should remain in or leave the European Union – called Brexit (Rotenberg, 2016).

The primary role of politicians is to persuade voters to endorse their views on everything and ultimately to vote for them (see Combs & Keller, 2010). The goal of their communication just happens to coincide with the conditions under which children and adults lie (see Chapter 2). Indeed, politicians engage in an exaggerated form of faking positivity in order to please others and attain approval. One way of undermining those effects is for the politician to present their communication as contrary to their self-interest – even compatible with the views of their opponents. This principle is supported by the study by Combs and Keller (2010). Their study was guided by the premise that a politician who engages in communications contrary to his or her self-interest violates expectations – in a positive fashion – which promotes perceptions of his or her trustworthiness.

In the first of three studies by those researchers, university undergraduates read an advertisement by a candidate (a fictional politician by the name of John Dixon) which was highly critical of his opponent (a fictional politician named David Hunter). The advertisement suggested that Hunter was a liar and that his policies would damage the state's economy. The undergraduates read one of three responses by David Hunter (all of which rejected the allegations at the onset): one went on to attack the moral values of his opponent (*counterattack*); one praised his own economic policies (*praised self*); and the third praised his opponent's policies as agreeing with his own and promised to take those forward to government if elected (*praised opponent*). It was found that the undergraduates judged the candidate as more trustworthy (i.e., showing trustworthiness, integrity, and honesty) and were more likely to vote for him when he had praised his opponent than when he counterattacked him. Furthermore, it was found that perceived trustworthiness was responsible, in part, for the pattern of voting. The three studies carried out by Combs and Keller (2010) provided support for the conclusion that people trust politicians and vote for them when they view the politician as acting against their own self-interest and positively violating expectations. From my perspective, this coincides with the principle that such acts decrease the likelihood that the politician is viewed as faking and thus deceiving others.

THE BDT FRAMEWORK

Guided by the BDT Framework, my colleagues and I (Rotenberg & Bierbrauer, in preparation) have examined trust beliefs in politicians. We have developed the Trust in Politicians (TP) Scale composed of scenarios that depict politicians potentially displaying three types of behaviour: reliability (e.g., keeping campaign promises), emotional trustworthiness (e.g., maintaining the confidentiality of information conveyed to government officials), and honesty (e.g., telling the truth about government spending). In our study, undergraduates were administered the TP scale and it was found, as expected, that the scale was composed of the three types of trust beliefs: reliability, emotional, and honesty. Also, we found that the undergraduates' honesty trust beliefs in politicians were associated with their willingness to vote for the Labour Party.

SUMMARY

The chapter began with the consideration of the Emperor's New Clothes story and its implications for the lack of trust in politicians today. The chapter reviews the research supporting the conclusion that some trust in government is essential for democracies and that trust is affected by international issues, economic issues, and political scandals. The chapter examined the attributes that potentially contribute to perceptions of politicians as trustworthy, such as acting against self-interest. Finally, the chapter culminates in the description of a BDT investigation of trust in politicians.

10

TERRORISM AND OUTGROUP DISTRUST

The Twin Towers and beyond

9/11 AND OTHER TERRORIST ACTS

Who can forget the images of the Twin Towers in New York being attacked on September 11, 2001 by planes controlled by Al-Qaeda terrorists? Al-Qaeda did later assume responsibility for the attacks (see CNN, November 14, 2015). The dreadful memory of 9/11 is etched into the minds of millions of people, including my own. Indeed, the image of the Twin Towers has become an icon and it may be regarded as a tragic symbol of subsequent terrorist acts. For example, an apparent al-Qaeda terrorist attack was carried out against a Madrid commuter train system on the morning of March 11, 2004, which killed 191 people and wounded around 2,000. There was a terrorist attack in Paris on Friday, November 13, 2015, which killed 130 and injured 368. Responsibility for the attacks was claimed by Islamic State of Iraq and the Levant (ISIL) (CNN, 2015). A terrorist attack was carried out in Brussels on Tuesday, March 22, 2016, which killed 31 and injured 300. It was apparently guided by the ISIL organisation.

This chapter on terrorism is guided by the following premises and hypotheses. First, the chapter is guided by the premise that terrorism is a distinct form of warfare that represents the convergence of untrustworthiness and aggression. Conventional warfare involves opponents meeting in open conflict. Aside from spying on the enemy, conventional warfare involves identifiable soldiers who bear the consequences of direct confrontation. By contrast, terrorism is subversive aggression integrated with highly untrustworthy behaviours such deceit, lying, and destructive malevolence. The primary target of this form of warfare is unprepared and undefended citizens – innocent victims.

Second, this chapter is guided by the hypothesis that outgroup distrust contributes to and shapes the majority of terrorist acts. Outgroup distrust refers to individuals' lack of trust in others who are perceived to be from a different group, typically identified by race, religion, political beliefs, and economic beliefs (Chambers & Melnyk, 2006; Voci, 2006). Third, and finally, guided by the preceding, it is proposed that terrorism results in increases in the recipient country's outgroup distrust in groups external to the country (e.g., countries related to the terrorism and potential immigrants into the country) and groups internal to the country (e.g., landed immigrants and ethnic minorities).

It should be highlighted here that it is difficult to know the identities or affiliations of the perpetrators of terrorism because they do not normally wear uniforms and often do not have an explicit chain of command. Even when a given terrorist group declares responsibility for an act it may be a falsehood to garner support for its cause. Even when evidence has accumulated to show that a given terrorist group has perpetrated the act, the lack of explicit chain of command can obscure that a given terrorist organisation was responsible for it. The reputation of the terrorist organisation may be sufficient to elicit the expected sequence as part of what is known as a self-fulfilling prophecy. Peoples' expectation that a terrorist act was perpetrated by a racial and political organisation (e.g., Al-Qaeda) alone could cause outgoup distrust and intergroup hostilities, which, in turn, would confirm the original biased expectation. These issues warrant careful consideration when reviewing the research on the topic.

The issue of terrorism bears on whether trust is solely linked to cooperative/beneficial outcomes as opposed to competitive/conflictual outcomes. Various approaches postulate that trust is dependent upon or promotes cooperative/beneficial outcomes (see sections on Social Capital, Game Theory, and Social Contact and Exchange Theories in Chapter 1). Nevertheless, some research shows that trust and co-operation are different constructs that are reciprocally associated (see Chapter 8). It would be unlikely for people to regard opponents in war as truly trustworthy even if they kept their promises and did other trust-worthy behaviours. Constraints on trusting opposing nations in any conventional war are imposed because people tend to view opponents as having some malicious intentions because they are an outgroup. Nevertheless, terrorism is a truly sinister act because the aggression is characterised by deceit, lying, and destructive malevolence.

A SOCIAL IDENTITY PERSPECTIVE ON 9/11 AND OTHER TERRORIST ACTS

An insight into terrorism is provided by Social Identity Theory, which was established by Tajfel and his colleagues (see Tajfel, 1981). According to SIT, individuals are naturally inclined to self-categorise people into an ingroup (us) vs outgroup (them). According to SIT, the ingroup seeks to distinguish itself from the outgroup by attributing negative distinctions to them or by bolstering the positive aspects of the ingroup. The Minimal group paradigm was employed to examine SIT. For example, Billig and Taifel (1972) had children allocate rewards to peers who were described as liking the same pictures as them (ingroup) or who were distinguished by no such information. In addition, the peers were further labelled as being part of their own group (ingroup) or not their own group (outgroup). It was found that the children showed high levels of ingroup favouritism by giving more points/money to ingroup members than outgroup members. Researchers have since refined and extended Social Identity Theory (e.g., Degner, Essien, & Reichardt, 2016).

Similar ingroup vs outgroup tendencies are evident in natural relationships such as relations between different racial, religious, and political groups (see Turner, Hogg, Oakes, Reicher, & Wetherell, 1987). It has been found that individuals perceive outgroup members (e.g. different race, culture, and political affiliation) as less trustworthy than ingroup members (Chambers & Melnyk, 2006; Voci, 2006). My colleagues and I (Rotenberg & Cerda, 1994) found outgroup distrust in both Native and non-Native elementary school children from Canada. The children believed that a hypothetical child would be less likely to keep promises, keep secrets, and be honest when he or she was of the different race than when he or she was of the same race. The pattern of outgoup distrust was stronger in children who were from same-race than mixed race schools. These findings highlighted the principle that social contact with other races promotes trust in them (also see Marschall & Stolle, 2004).

The study by Chambers and Melnyk (2006, study 2) demonstrates the role of outgroup distrust in political affiliation with university students. The researchers found that students who were Democrats were more likely to view Republican undergraduates as having negative traits, including dishonesty and untrustworthiness, than students who were also Democrats. Similarly, students who were Republicans were more likely to view Democratic undergraduates as having negative traits (including dishonesty and untrustworthiness) than did students who were also Republicans. Furthermore, the students perceived that there were more disagreements between them and those opinions of their rivals than actually existed; and that those opinions were more central to the beliefs than they actually were. Chambers and Melnyk (2006) argued that racial discrimination and hostility were products of outgroup distrust, perceived exaggeration of differences in values, and the exaggeration of the centrality of those conflicting values.

Living in a racial heterogeneity has the potential to promote trust in outgroup members by increasing social contact with other races. In support of that hypothesis, Marschall and Stolle (2004) found that neighbourhood racial heterogeneity (i.e., mixed racial communities) in Detroit had a positive effect on Black people's generalised trust. Black people who resided in a mixed racial neighbourhood held more elevated generalised trust beliefs in others than did those who resided in a uniracial neighbourhood.

POST 9/11: SHORT-TERM "EFFECTS" OF TRUST IN THE GOVERNMENT

The term "effects" is placed in quotation marks in this chapter because it is very difficult to identify with any certainty the causes and consequences of a single incident such as 9/11. This issue warrants consideration when reviewing the research. Studies on this topic utilise data from nationwide surveys (e.g., American National Election Studies) that require citizens to rate on a scale the measure of their trust in government (e.g., trust that government will do what is right). The findings yield some support for the conclusion that the American public's trust in government increased after 9/11. It rose from 29 percent in March 2001 to 64 percent in late September 2001 (Chanley, 2002; Skocpol, 2002). One account of this phenomenon is that people rally in support of their government when they perceive a threat to their survival (see Woods, 2011) and this may be viewed as an effect of outgroup distrust. The 9/11 attack caused a temporary increase in the salience of Americans' ingroup identification (us vs them) which would have the effect of bolstering their trust in their ingroup comprising their fellow Americans and the US government.

Rather provocatively, individuals adhering to conspiracy theories believe that government agencies and representatives have colluded on or facilitated the 9/11 terrorist act. They believe that the government engages in this sort of action for the purposes of clamping down on civil liberties and promoting involvement in foreign wars (i.e., those in Afghanistan and Iraq). Swami, Chamorro-Premuzic, and Furnham (2010) tested 254 UK women and men and found that those who held conspiracy beliefs regarding 9/11 believed in other conspiracy theories and had heightened exposure to 9/11 conspiracist ideas. Furthermore, that group of individuals showed elevated political cynicism, elevated defiance of authority, and low agreeableness personality. The findings highlight the role of social exposure to ideas and oppositional personality as factors contributing to holding a conspiracy theory regarding 9/11.

POST 9/11: LONG-TERM "EFFECTS" OF TRUST IN THE GOVERNMENT

Although trust in government remained high for three to five months after 9/11, it *appears* to be short lived. Brewer, Aday, and Gross (2005) assessed trust at three times (waves) in an initial sample of 1,235 US citizens from 2001 through to 2002. It was found that there were decreases across time in political trust. This finding supports the conclusion that Americans' trust in government returned to pre-9/11 levels or below those levels.

THE "EFFECTS" OF 9/11 AND OTHER TERRORIST ACTS ON TRUST IN OTHERS

In support of the hypothesis guiding this chapter, there are a variety of events indicative of a decrease in trust in other nations and other races since 9/11. Brewer, Aday, and Gross (2005) found that international trust (i.e., believing that other nations would be helpful to the US) decreased. There have been reports that anti-immigrant prejudice has increased in the US and in Europe since 9/11 (Ceobanu & Escandell, 2008). Although the evidence is very limited, hate crimes against Muslims appear to have increased in the US and other Western countries since 9/11 as well as subsequent terrorist acts (see Arora, 2013; also see Bushman & Bonacci, 2004). The national and racial tensions resulting from 9/11 are shown in the subsequent increases in security measures in Western countries. As expected, monitoring and securitising travellers, communications, and international financial transactions have increased. In addition, some authors have observed a reduction in the rights of foreigners since 9/11, which has been a source of ethical concern (Crépeau & Jimenez, 2004).

The problem with explicit measures of prejudice is that they are obvious, and people are reluctant to endorse prejudice on the measures because it is socially undesirable to do so. For that reason, social psychologists have developed implicit tests of prejudice that avoid the effects of social desirability (see the shooter task in Chapter 7, page 55). Bushman and Bonacci (2004) used a lost e-mail letter method as an implicit test of prejudice towards Arabs in the US. These researchers administered standardised measures of explicit prejudice to 140 European-American US college students. Those students later received a misaddressed (i.e., lost) e-mail which was intended for an Arab or a European-American. The e-mail stated that the intended recipient either had or had not received a prestigious four-year college scholarship (scholarship success vs failure, respectively). The e-mail further stated that a reply was required within 24 hours. The researchers found a main effect of ethnic identity: the college students were less likely to reply to the e-mail when the intended recipient was Arab than when he or she was European-American. Those effects were qualified, however, by the success of the scholarship and prejudice of the participants. Low-prejudice students (on the standardised explicit measures) were just as likely to reply to a lost e-mail pertaining to scholarship success for Arab and European-American recipients. The pattern was quite different for students with high prejudice, however. High-prejudice students were less likely to reply to the e-mail pertaining to *scholarship success* when the intended recipient was Arab. When the e-mail pertained to *scholarship failure*, though, high-prejudice students showed the opposite ethnic bias, and were more likely to reply when the intended recipient was Arab. The findings demonstrate an overall prejudice – in a passive fashion – against Arabs by US students: they were less inclined to reply to a lost e-mail intended for an Arab than European-American. The findings show, though, that prejudicial attitudes play a role in discriminatory behaviour towards Arabs. The highly prejudiced students showed evidence of engaging in active harmful behaviour (i.e., insulting) towards Arabs.

SUMMARY

This chapter begins with a consideration of the 9/11 attack and other terrorist attacks. The chapter reviewed the research, which yielded some support for the hypothesis that outgroup distrust contributes to terrorism and that outgroup distrust is a consequence of terrorism. The chapter reviewed the research indicating that trust in government increased after the 9/11 terrorist attack but it was temporary.

11

TRUST AND RELIGIOUS FAITH

Do we trust God?

The book of Exodus in the Bible depicts Moses as leading the Israelites from captivity in Egypt to salvation in the Promised Land. It depicts people, who had been slaves, learning to trust God and his word. Learning to trust God is the foundation of many religions. The purpose of this chapter is to review the research on trust in God.

KNOWLEDGE ACQUISITION THEORY (KAT)

The supreme deity is unseen and therefore individuals who believe in this deity need to trust that the deity exists across time and in the future. Harris (2007) articulated this principle in the KAT in the form of children acquiring those beliefs because of their trust in others. Further implications of the KAT for religion were examined by Corriveau, Chen, and Harris (2015). They investigated children's differentiation between real and pretend as a function of religiosity of family background. The research supported the hypothesis that religious upbringing predisposes young children to use religious beliefs to decide whether religious events are real, and fantastic events are real rather than pretend.

ATTACHMENT THEORY

God as an attachment figure is the core principle in the Attachment Theory conceptualisation of trust in God (Kirkpatrick, 1992; also see Chapters 1, 4, and 5 in this book). Granqvist, Mikulincer, Gewirtz, and Shaver (2012) found support for the hypothesis that individuals generalised their security of interpersonal attachments, via their Internal Working Model of caregiver-child relationship, to the quality of their attachment to God. The studies showed that individuals with a secure quality of interpersonal attachment demonstrated a secure quality of attachment to God and thus regarded him as a secure base and haven from distress. Those individuals were inclined to view God as loving, sensitive, reliable, and warm. By the same token, individuals with insecure/avoidant interpersonal attachment tended have an insecure quality of attachment to God and failed to view him as a secure base and view him as distant or controlling. Implicit priming methods were used in other studies by Granqvist et al. (2012) and the findings further showed that those attachment processes work at a nonconscious level.

A BDT FRAMEWORK

From the Bases, Domains, and Target Dimensions (BDT) Framework perspective, adherence to a religion requires that individuals believe that the deity and religious leaders fulfil their promises such an afterlife (reliability) and will listen to confessions and prayers with compassion (emotional trustworthiness). Also, individuals are required to believe the deity and religious leaders are truthful, genuine, and guided by benign intentions (honesty). Those beliefs are manifested in the behavioural dependence by individuals in the form of following religious practices. Also, the deity and religious leaders expect individuals to reciprocate (in a form) by keeping their promises such as to attend church (reliability), listening to religious leaders guided by acceptance and sincerity (emotional trustworthiness), and telling the truth notably to religious leaders (honesty). In support of this proposal, religious leaders have advocated precisely this form of trust in God in order to promote religion in contemporary society (see Moltmann, 2006).

ROSMARIN'S APPROACH TO TRUST AND RELIGION

Rosmarin and his colleagues (Rosmarin, Krumrei et al., 2009; Rosmarin, Pargament et al., 2009; Rosmarin, Pargament, Pirutinsky, & Mahoney, 2010) constructed a Brief Trust in God (called the TMIG) scale. This scale is composed of two subscales: a trust in God (TIG) subscale (e.g., belief in God as compassionate) and a mistrust in God (MIG) subscale (i.e., belief in God as often being unkind). The research supports the conclusion that the TIG and MIG items/subscales are separate but associated constructs, and that each subscale demonstrates adequate internal consistency. The TMIG was developed to assess trust in God in Western countries, notably for Christians and Jews. The TMIG has been adjusted for use in Islamic countries, specifically for Muslims (Hafizi, Rosmarin, & Koenig, 2014).

DOES RELIGIOSITY AFFECT INDIVIDUALS' TRUST IN OTHERS?

Researchers have examined whether there are "effects" of religiosity on various forms of trust. Organised religion serves to establish boundaries of ingroup vs outgroup that affect trust – resulting in outgroup distrust (see Chapter 10). As support for this hypothesis, Fitzgerald and Wickwire (2012) engaged university students in a trust game with partners identified as having the same religious affiliation as theirs or a different one (i.e., Baptist or Catholic). Trust choice was assessed by what share of £10 the students (as a first player) would provide to the other player (second player) who could then divide the total sum of monies between them (see Chapter 1). It was found that the students demonstrated greater trust choice when playing with the partner who had the same religious affiliation (i.e., ingroup member) than different religious affiliation (i.e., outgroup member).

Religion-based outgroup distrust has been examined further by Ward, Mamerow, and Meyer (2014) in a sample of 6,331 individuals who were residents in the countries of Taiwan, Hong Kong, South Korea, Japan, Australia, and Thailand. The persons were asked to rate how much they trusted family, neighbours, strangers, foreigners, and people with a different religion. The researchers found that reported trust in family and neighbours was very high across all the six countries. There were differences between countries in the citizens' trust in people with a different religion. Trust in persons with a different religion was highest for citizens of Australia, Hong Kong, and Taiwan, and lowest for citizens of Japan, South Korea, and Thailand.

The role that religion plays in generalised trust others has been examined by Olson and Miao (2015). These researchers carried out multilevel analyses of the World Values Survey data that were gathered from 77,409 citizens in 69 countries. The countries ranged from Albania to Vietnam. The analyses examined the extent to which generalised social trust is related to the percent of the population that is religious and the religious heterogeneity of a country. Generalised social trust was assessed by the willingness of individuals to trust most people (see Chapter 1). National religious participation was measured by the proportion of people who reported they attended religious services at least once a month (apart from weddings, funerals, and festivities). Religious heterogeneity was derived from estimations of the sizes of each religious group based on the proportion of respondents in each group for that country. It was found that the percent of the population who were religious was negatively associated with generalised social trust: the greater the percent of a country that was religious then the less the citizens held generalised trust in others. Furthermore, the researchers found that generalised social trust was very low (about one-half of the average) when countries had a combination of higher-than-average religiosity and higher-than-average religious heterogeneity. As one account of the findings, the authors proposed that people from countries that emerged from competing and strong religious backgrounds are unwilling to trust those with other religions and others in general. This is consistent with Social Identity Theory (see Chapter 10), because the strength of social identity would promote outgroup distrust in those countries.

DOES TRUST IN GOD PROMOTE PSYCHOLOGICAL ADJUSTMENT AND HEALTH?

Rosmarin and his colleagues (e.g., Rosmarin, Pirutinsky, & Pargament, 2011) have proposed that trust as opposed to distrust in God promotes positive spiritual coping, religious coping, a sense of connectedness, and a sense of transcendence. It was proposed that individuals who trust (rather than mistrust) God are therefore more willing to tolerate uncertainty, which serves to reduce the likelihood of worrying and experiencing anxiety. As evidence for these hypotheses, Rosmarin et al. (2011) found that individuals' mistrust in God was positively associated with worry and that was due, in part, to their lack of tolerance of uncertainty. Similarly, individuals' trust in God was negatively associated with worry, and that was due, in part, to their tolerance of uncertainty.

Breast cancer is the most common form of cancer in Black women, and the second most common cause of death among Black women. The church is a cornerstone of life for Black women and that faith could help them cope with serious illnesses such as cancer. Guided by these principles, Beverly, Yoo, and Levine (2014) carried out in-depth interviews with 47 Black women about their experiences with their treatment for breast cancer. The participants were posed a series of open-ended questions regarding the role of religious and spiritual practices, from diagnosis to surviving cancer. The women's answers were transcribed and subjected to qualitative analyses to reveal the common themes. The majority of the women mentioned using both individual and communal religious and spiritual practices to cope with their breast cancer diagnosis and treatment. These included attendance at religious services, comfort through prayers of others, and reading Biblical scriptures. The researchers argued that the women's "trust in the Lord" helped them to cope with cancer and survive the illness. It was proposed that clinicians incorporate religion and spirituality into the treatment of individuals, notably Black women, to assist them in coping with their illnesses. This study is interesting because it highlights the potential role that trust in God plays in coping with serious illnesses such as cancer.

SUMMARY

The chapter included a description of the role of trust in religion from the perspectives of KAT, Attachment Theory, and the BDT Framework. The chapter reviewed the research on trust in religion by Rosmarin and his colleagues and the potential benefits that trust may have on psychological adjustment and physical health.

12

BUILDING TRUST

The consequences of lying, betrayal, unseen facets of distrust, and terrorism have been described in previous chapters of this book. How can trust be promoted or violations of trust be repaired? In contrast to the breadth of research on trust, there are a very limited number of strategies/interventions within the discipline of psychology for promoting trust or repairing violations of it. This chapter will review the existing research on the topic.

BUILDING TRUST BETWEEN OPPOSING NATIONS

One of the earliest strategies for promoting trust between opposing nations was developed by Osgood (1962). He was concerned with the Cold War and the arms race during 1960s. He recommended that nations engage in a strategy of graduated reciprocity in tension reduction (GRIT) as a means to disarmament. According to GRIT, disarmament between two nations can be conceptualised as two partners in a mixed-motive game. The strategy involves the first partner (a nation) making a modest reduction in arms that is verifiable. The partner then waits until the other partner reciprocates by a similar reduction in arms. Next, the first partner engages in a greater reduction in arms that is then reciprocated by the other player. As a consequence of the reciprocated exchanges of verifiable actions, a trusting relationship emerges between the partners (nations) and mutual disarmament is achieved. The GRIT proposal and its psychological underpinnings has been described in some detail by Lindskold (1978). His review highlights the significance of building objective credibility and the attributions of trustworthiness in the exchanges proposed by GRIT to achieve disarmament between countries. Although GRIT is a promising strategy for building trust between opposing nations and disarmament, its effectiveness remains to be shown.

GRIT has served as an impetus for trust-promoting interventions. For example Cook et al. (2005) employed a version of the Prisoners' Dilemma (PD) game that permitted separation of the willingness to risk and cooperation. The PD/R (R for risk) comprised an exchange of coins between two players in which one player chose the number of coins he or she gave to a partner (entrusting them to him or her) and the other player chose the amount of coins he or she gave in return. Risk and thus trust was assessed by the number of coins a player gave/entrusted to the other player and cooperation was the number of coins the other player returned. Cook et al. (2005) carried out three experiments using that method. The studies support the conclusions that risk-taking was a critical element in trust-building, and Americans are more willing to take risks than are Japanese.

BUILDING TRUST BETWEEN PEOPLE WITH DIFFERENT RELIGIONS

Outgroup distrust regarding religion poses a threat to society, especially for those countries with strongly religious citizens and heterogeneity of religion (see Chapter 11, Olson & Miao, 2015). Northern Ireland (NI) is such a country. Hewstone and his colleagues (Hewstone, 2015; Tam, Hewstone, Kenworthy, & Cairns, 2009; Turner, Tam, Hewstone, Kenworthy, & Cairns, 2013; Turner et al., 2010) have examined the hypothesis that cross-religious group contact contributes to trust and positive relationships between religious groups in NI. NI is composed of 44% Catholic and 53% Protestant citizens. Many Catholic citizens of NI believe that it should leave the UK whereas many of the Protestant citizens of NI want it to remain in the UK. Considerable progress has been made in promoting religious acceptance and tolerance in NI over the last decades but a degree of religious polarisation and outgroup distrust remain. In their research, Hewstone and his colleagues have drawn upon the Social Contact Theory established by Allport (1954; see Pettigrew, 1998) which prescribes that positive social interaction with outgroup members, notably equal-status relationships, promotes trust and positive relationships between ethnic minorities and majorities and thus decreases prejudice and hostility.

In one study Tam, Hewstone, Kenworthy, and Cairns (2009, Study 2) tested 175 young Catholics and Protestants from three large universities in NI. The undergraduate students completed an outgroup distrust scale (e.g., "I can't trust them because they want revenge for things we have done to them", p. 47). The students reported the quantity of their contact with the outgroup (i.e., people of a different religion) and the quality of their contact with the outgroup (e.g., pleasantness and cooperativeness of those contacts). Also, the students reported their extended contact with the outgroup, such having being close friends, or knowing their families. The students reported their positive behavioural tendencies towards the outgroup, such as approaching them, and negative behavioural tendencies – to avoid the outgroup. The students reported their outgroup attitudes in the form of the outgroup being warm vs cold, negative vs positive, friendly vs hostile. Finally, the students completed a scale assessing their opportunity for contact, such as living near them.

The findings confirmed that both the quantity and quality of intergroup interaction statistically predicted trust in the religious outgroup, which statistically predicted positive behavioural tendencies towards the religious outgroup. These findings supported the hypothesis that individuals' social contact with outgroup religious members promotes their trust in the religious outgroup, which, in turn, promotes positive behavioural tendencies towards them. As expected, positive behavioural tendencies towards the outgroup were associated with outgroup attitudes, extended contact, and the opportunity of contact. Similar intergroup interaction patterns have been found in young children residing in NI (Turner, Tam, Hewstone, Kenworthy, & Cairns, 2013).

BUILDING TRUST BETWEEN PARENTS AND CHILDREN

Strategies for parents promoting children's trust in them have been discussed in Chapter 4. In that vein, Colonnesi et al. (2012) have investigated the effectiveness of attachment-oriented intervention, called Basic Trust, to promote positive parent-child relationships in families with adopted children. Families with adopted children were targeted because those children were regarded as at high risk for insecure attachment relationships arising from adverse preadoption conditions, such as institutional rearing. The Basic Trust intervention was designed to promote and improve parental-mindedness (i.e., being aware of childrens' minds) by teaching parents to objectively attend to their children's behaviours and signals by engaging in a specific communication skill (called mental state discourse). Parents were engaged in naming the behaviours, feelings, wishes, intentions, and thoughts of the child. The practice of naming was designed to promote attachment security in children particularly for the purpose of making the child feel accepted as a person. In the study, parents from 20 Dutch families with adopted children (2–5 years of age) were engaged in eight Basic Trust method training sessions. The parents' sensitivity and children's attachment were assessed by observations of their interactions in a research room and during a family meal. The children's attachment insecurity and psychopathology were assessed by parents' completion of standardised measures. The researchers reported that there were decreases from pretest to posttest (3 months later): in insecurity of attachment as reported by mothers, disorganised attachment as reported by parents, and conduct problems as reported by parents. The Basic Trust intervention is a promising strategy for improving parent-child relationships, but the findings regarding its effectiveness are uncertain. For example, the design lacked a no-treatment control group and therefore it is unclear whether the observed changes are due to the Basic Trust training rather than to other factors such as repeated testing or time.

BUILDING TRUST WITHIN A PERSON

The psychosocial problems that beset individuals with low trust have been described in Chapter 3. Low trust is associated with psychosocial problems such as loneliness, aggression, and low cooperation with others. Based on these findings it would be useful to develop a therapy to promote low-trust individuals' trust beliefs in others. It is important to recognise here that instilling patients' belief that the therapist is trustworthy (e.g., keeps promises, keeps secrets, and is honest) is the cornerstone of most forms of therapy (see Laughton-Brown, 2010). For person-centred therapy in particular, the effectiveness of the therapy depends on the client holding high emotional trust beliefs which comprise the expectation that the therapist uncritically accepts personal disclosure and maintains confidentiality of it (see Thorne, 2007).

Research has shown that priming trust cognitions by required word recall promotes trust beliefs and social engagement (see Rotenberg, 2010; Study 4). If priming was integrated into Cognitive Behavioural Therapy (CBT) it could serve as a treatment for those individuals with low trust beliefs. Clients who have low trust beliefs in others and show concomitant psychosocial problems would be prompted during therapy to generate trusting cognitions as part of imagined social interactions. Guided by the therapist, the clients would be taught to self-prompt those trusting cognitions during real-life social interactions following the therapy sessions. The therapist would need to be mindful in this intervention of the potential consequences of trusting too much and of the objective trustworthiness of others in the clients' social relationships. As support for this suggested intervention, there are case studies in which CBT has been focused on changing trust-related cognitions as a treatment for paranoia (Smith & Steel, 2009).

BUILDING TRUST WITH FUTURE GENERATIONS

Trust during later adulthood (55–75 years) and very old age (older than 75 years) includes the issues of family members' inheritance claims, and whether the trust placed in family members or mankind will be fulfilled (Rotenberg, 2015). This aspect of trust complements Erik Erikson's generativity vs stagnation conflict stage as it pertains to individuals' satisfaction in influencing and caring for future generations, including their own children (Erikson, 1963; Hamachek, 1990). This facet of trust warrants further investigation.

IS TRUST A CRISIS OR EVERYTHING?

The question of whether trust is a crisis or everything was posed at the onset of this book. This book provides material on a wide range of topics regarding trust, including parenting, health professionals, police, workplace, politicians, terrorism, and outgroups. Furthermore, the book has attempted to familiarise readers with the extensive range of research on the topic of trust. This coverage alone supports the conclusion that, although trust is not everything, it is truly a pervasive facet of modern life.

SUMMARY

This chapter addressed the issue of how trust could be promoted or violations of trust be repaired. It included a summary of research bearing on building trust between opposing nations (e.g., Osgood's GRIT proposal), different religions (e.g., Hewstone and his colleagues), between parents and their children (e.g., Colonnesi et al., 2012), within the person (as part of CBT), and between older adults and future generations. The chapter culminates in the confirmation that trust is an essential facet of our modern world.

FURTHER RESOURCES

READINGS

Trust in Schools: A Core Resource for Improvement (2002) by Anthony S. Bryk and Barbara Schneider, Russell Sage Foundation.

Trusting What You're Told: How Children Learn from Others (2012) by Paul L. Harris, Harvard University Press.

Trust: From Socrates to Spin (2004) by K. O'Hara, Cambridge University Press

Trust and Scepticism (2014) by Liz Robinson and Shiri Einav (Editors), Psychology Press.

FILMS

Title: Sex, Lies, and Videotape
Date/Type/Length: 1989/Comedy, Drama/1h 40min
Director: Steven Soderbergh
Screenplay: Steven Soderbergh
Stars: James Spader, Andie MacDowell, Peter Gallagher, Laura San Giacomo

Title: Trust
Date/Type/Length: 1991/Comedy, Drama/1h 47min
Director: Hal Hartley
Writer: Hal Hartley
Stars: Adrienne Shelly, Martin Donovan, Rebecca Nelson

Title: Trust Me
Date/Type/Length: 1991/Comedy, Drama/1h 47min
Director: Clark Gregg
Writer: Clark Gregg
Stars: Clark Gregg, Felicity Huffman, Allison Janne

Title: Simple Men
Date/Type/Length: 1992/Crime, Drama, Romance/1h 45min
Director: Hal Hartley
Writer: Hal Hartley
Stars: Robert John Burke, Bill Sage, Martin Donovan

Title: Broken Trust
Date/Type/Length: 1995/Thriller/1h 30min
Director: Geoffrey Sax
Writers: William P. Wood (novel), Joan Didion (teleplay)
Stars: Tom Selleck, Elizabeth McGovern, William Atherton

Title: Trust
Date/Type/Length: 2003/Crime, Drama/1h 57min
Director: Parris Reaves
Writers: William Pierce, Fred Spivey
Stars: Eric Lane, Dori Torel

Title: Trust the Man
Date/Type/Length: 2005/Comedy, Drama, Romance/1h 43min
Director: Bart Freundlich
Writer: Bart Freundlich
Stars: David Duchovny, Julianne Moore, Billy Crudup

Title: Trust
Date/Type/Length: 2010/Thriller, Drama/1h 44min
Director: David Schwimmer
Screenplay: Andy Bellin, Rob Festinger
Stars: Clive Owen, Liana Liberato

TV SERIES

Trust (TV series). A legal drama created by Simon Block and written by Simon Block and Andrew Rattenbury.

REFERENCES

Ainsworth, M. D. S. (1989). Attachments beyond infancy. *American Psychologist*, 44, 709–716.

Alcock, J. (2001). *Animal behavior: An evolutionary approach* (7th ed.). Sunderland, MA: Sinauer Associates.

Allport, G. W. (1954). *The nature of prejudice*. Reading, MA: Addison-Wesley.

Anderson, L. A., & Dedrick, R. F. (1990). Development of the trust in physician scale: A measure to assess interpersonal trust in patient-physician relationships. *Psychological Reports*, 67, 1091–1100.

Arora, K. S. K. (2013). Reflections on the experiences of turbaned Sikh men in the aftermath of 9/11. *Journal for Social Action in Counseling & Psychology*, 5(1), 116–121.

Baker, A. J. L. (2005). The long-term effects of parental alienation on adult children: A qualitative research study. *American Journal of Family Therapy*, 33(4), 289–302. doi: 10.1080/01926180590962129

Barefoot, J. C., Maynard, K. E., Beckham, J. C., Brammett, B. H., Hooker, K., & Siegler, I. C. (1998). Trust, health and longevity. *Journal of Behavioral Medicine*, 21, 517–526.

Baron, R. A., & Neuman, J. H. (1996). Workplace violence and workplace aggression: Evidence on their relative frequency and potential causes. *Aggressive Behavior*, 22, 161–173.

Baron, R. A., Neuman, J. H., & Geddes, D. (1999). Social and personal determinants of workplace aggression: Evidence for the impact of perceived injustice and the Type A Behavior Pattern. *Aggressive Behaviour*, 25(4), 281–296.

Benner, J. A. (2004). Biblical word of the month – Trust in ancient Hebrew research center. *Biblical Hebrew E-Magazine* Issue #010. Retrieved from www.ancient-hebrew.org/emagazine/010.html

Beverly, L. Yoo, G. J., & Levine, E. G. (2014). "Trust in the Lord": Religious and spiritual practices of African American breast cancer survivors *Journal of Religious Health*, 53, 1706–1716. doi:10.1007/s10943-013-9750-x

Billig, M., & Tajfel, H. (1972). Social categorization and similarity in intergroup behavior. *European Journal of Social Psychology*, 3, 27–52.

Birkhäuer, J., Gaab, J., Kossowsky, J., Hasler, S., Krummenacher, P., Werner, C., & Gerger, H. (2017). Trust in the health care professional and health outcome: A meta-analysis. *PLoS ONE*, 12(2), 1–13. doi:10.1371/journal.pone.0170988

Birnie-Porter, C., & Hunt, M. (2015). Does relationship status matter for sexual satisfaction? The roles of intimacy and attachment avoidance in sexual satisfaction across five types of ongoing sexual relationships. *Canadian Journal of Human Sexuality*, 24(2), 174–183. doi:10.3138/cjhs.242-A5

Blendon, R. J., Benson, J. M., & Hero, J. O. (2014). Public trust in physicians – U.S. medicine in international perspective. *New England Journal of Medicine*, 371, 1570–1572. doi:10.1056/NEJMp1407373

Blind, P. K. (2007). Building trust in government in the twenty-first century: Review of literature and emerging issues. *7th Global Forum on Reinventing Government*, 26–29 June, Vienna Austria.

Bond, C. F., & DePaulo, B. M. (2006). Accuracy of deception judgments. *Personality and Social Psychology Review*, 10, 214–234. doi:10.1207/s15327957pspr1003_2

Bond, C. F., & DePaulo, B. M. (2008). Individual differences in judging deception: Accuracy and bias. *Psychological Bulletin*, 134, 477–492. doi:10.1037/0033-2909.134.4.477

Bowlby, J. (1980). *Loss: Sadness & Depression*. Attachment and Loss (Vol. 3). London: Hogarth.

Brewer, P. R., Aday, S., & Gross, K. (2005). Do Americans trust other nations? A panel study. *Social Science Quarterly*, 86(1), 36–51. 10.1111/j.0038-4941.2005.00289.x

British Crime Survey for England and Wales. (2009–2010). National Statistics, Home Office Statistical Bulletin.

Bryk, A. S., & Schneider, B. (2002). *Trust in schools: A core resource for improvement*. New York: The American Sociological Association's Rose Series in Sociology, Russell Sage Foundation.

Bushman, B. J., & Bonacci, A. M. (2004). You've got mail: Using e-mail to examine the effects of prejudiced attitudes on discrimination against Arabs. *Journal of Experimental Social Psychology*, 40, 753–759. doi:10.1016/j.jesp.2004.02.001

Buss, D. M., Larsen, R. J., Westen, D., & Semmelroth, J. (1992). Sex differences in jealousy: Evolution, physiology, and psychology. *Psychological Science*, 3, 251–255.

Cambridge University Dictionary. Retrieved from http://dictionary.cambridge.org/dictionary/english/trust

Ceobanu, A. M., & Escandell, X. (2008). East is West? National feelings and anti-immigrant sentiment in Europe. *Social Science Research*, 37(4), 1147–1170.

Chaitin, E., Stiller, R., Jacobs, S., Hershl, J., Grogen, T., & Weinberg, J. (2003). Physician-patient relationship in the intensive care unit: Erosion of the sacred trust? *Critical CareMedicine*, 31, 367–372.

Chambers, J. R., & Melnyk, D. (2006). Why do I hate thee? Conflict misperceptions and intergroup mistrust. *Personality and Social Psychology Bulletin*, 32(10), 1295–1311. doi:http://dx.doi.org/10.1177/0146167206289979

Chanley, V. (2002). Trust in government in the aftermath of 9/11: Determinants and consequences. *Political Psychology*, 23(3), 469–483. doi: http://dx.doi.org/10.1111/0162-895X.00294

Cheng, H., Bynner, J., Wiggins, R., & Schoon, I. (2012). The measurement and evaluation of social attitudes in two British Cohort studies. *Social Research Council*, 107, 351–371.

CNN (2015). ISIS claims responsibility of Paris attacks. Retrieved November 14, 2015.

Cohn, D. (1990). Child-mother attachment of six-year-olds and social competence at school. *Child Development*, 61(1),152–162. doi: 10.1111/1467-8624.ep9102040550

Cohen-Charash, Y., & Spector, P. E. (2001). The role of justice in organizations: A meta-analysis. *Organizational Behavior and Human Decision Processes*, 86(2), 278–321. doi:10.1006/obhd.2001.2958

Collins, N. L., & Read, S. J. (1990). Adult attachment, working models, and relationship quality in dating couples. *Journal of Personality and Social Psychology*, 58, 644–663.

Colonnesi, C., Wissink, I. B., Noom, M. J., Asscher, J. J. Hoeve, M., Stams, G. J. J. M., Polderman, N., & Kellaert-Knol, M. G. (2012). Basic trust: An attachment-oriented intervention based on mind-mindedness in adoptive families. *Research on Social Work Practice*, 23(2), 179–188. doi:10.1177/1049731512469301

Combs, D. J. Y., & Keller, P. S. (2010). Politicians and trustworthiness: Acting contrary to self-interest enhances trustworthiness. *Basic and Applied Social Psychology*, 32, 328–339. doi:10.1080/01973533.2010.519246

Cook, J., & Wall, T. D. (1980). New work attitude measures of trust, organizational commitment and personal need-nonfulfillment. *Journal of Occupational Psychology*, 53, 39–52.

Cook, K. S., Yamagishi, T., Cheshire, C., Cooper, R., Matsuda, M., & Mashima, R. (2005). Trust building via risk taking: A cross-societal experiment. *Social Psychology Quarterly*, 68(2), 121–142.

Corbacho, A., Philipp, J., & Ruiz-Vega, M. (2015). Crime and erosion of trust: Evidence for Latin America. *World Development*, 70, 400–415. doi:10.1016/j.worlddev.2014.04.013

Correll, J., Hudson, S. M., Guillermo, S., & Ma, D. S. (2014). The police officer's dilemma: A decade of research on racial bias in the decision to shoot. *Social and Personality Psychology Compass*, 8, 201–213. doi:http://dx.doi.org/10.1111/spc3.12099.

Corriveau, K. H., Chen, E. E., & Harris, P. L. (2015). Judgments about fact and fiction by children from religious and nonreligious backgrounds. *Cognitive Science*, 39(2), 353–382. doi:10.1111/cogs.12138

Cozzolino, P. J. (2011). Trust, cooperation, and equality: A psychological analysis of the formation of social capital. *British Journal of Social Psychology*, 50(2), 302–320. doi:10.1348/014466610X519610

Crane, F. (1935). As quoted in *Business Education World*, 15, 172.

Crépeau, F., & Jimenez, E. (2004). Foreigners and the right to justice in the aftermath of 9/11. *International Journal of Law and Psychiatry*, 27(6), Special Issue: Migration, mental health, and human rights, 609–626. doi:http://dx.doi.org/10.1016/j.ijlp.2004.08.002

Crossman, A. M., & Lewis, M. (2006). Adults' ability to detect children's lying. *Behavioral Sciences and the Law*, 24, 703–715. doi:10.1002/bsl.731

Degner, J., Essien, I., & Reichardt, R. (2016). Effects of diversity versus segregation on automatic approach and avoidance behavior towards own and other ethnic groups. *European Journal of Social Psychology*, 46(6), 783–791. doi:10.1002/ejsp.2234

DePaulo, B. M., Ansfield, M. E., Kirkendol, S. E., & Boden, J. M. (2004). Serious lies. *Basic and Applied Social Psychology*, 26(2–3), 147–167. doi:http://dx.doi.org/10.1207/s15324834basp2602&3_4

DePaulo, B. M., & Kashy, D. A. (1998). Everyday lies in close and casual relationships. *Journal of Personality and Social Psychology*, 74(1), 63–79. doi:http://dx.doi.org/10.1037/0022-3514.74.1.63

DePaulo, B. M., Kashy, D. A., Kirkendol, S. E., Wyer, M. M., & Epstein, J. A. (1996). Lying in everyday life. *Journal of Personality and Social Psychology*, 70, 979–995.

DePaulo, B. M., Lanier, K., & Davis, T. (1983). Detecting the deceit of the motivated liar. *Journal of Personality and Social Psychology*, 45(5), 1096–1103. doi:http://dx.doi.org/10.1037/0022-3514.45.5.1096

DePaulo, B. M., Lindsay, J. L., Malone, B. E., Muhlenbruck, L., Charlton, K., & Cooper, H. (2003). Cues to deception. *Psychological Bulletin*, 129, 74–118. doi:10.1037/0033-2909.129.1.74.

Deutsch, M. (1958). Trust and suspicion. *Journal of Conflict Resolution*, 2, 265–279.

Edelman, R. (2015, November 2). *A crisis of trust: A warning to both business and government*. Retrieved from www.theworldin.com/article/10508/crisis-trust?fsrc=scn%2Ffb%2Fte%2Fbl%2Fed%2Ftheworldin2016

Erikson, E. H. (1963). *Childhood and society* (2nd ed.). New York: Norton.

Fairburn, C. G., & Harrison, P. J. (2003). Eating disorders. *Lancet*, 361(9355), 407–417.

Feeney, J. A., & Noller, P. (1990). Attachment style as a predictor of adult romantic relationships. *Journal of Personality and Social Psychology*, 58, 281–291.

Ferrin, D. L., Bligh, M. C., & Kohles, J. C. (2008). It takes two to tango: An interdependence analysis of the spiralling of perceived trustworthiness and cooperation in interpersonal and intergroup relationships. *Organizational Behavior and Human Decision Processes*, 107(2), 161–178. doi:http://dx.doi.org/10.1016/j.obhdp.2008.02.012

Fisher, J., van Heerde, J., & Tucker, A. (2010). Does one trust judgment fit all? Linking theory and empirics. *The British Journal of Politics and International Relations*, 12, 161–188. doi:10.1111/j.1467-856X.2009.00401.x

Fitzgerald, C. J., & Wickwire, J. H. (2012). Religion and political affiliation's influence on trust and reciprocity among strangers. *Journal of Social, Evolutionary & Cultural Psychology*, 6(2), 158–180.

Flanagan, C. A., & Stout, M. (2010). Developmental patterns of social trust between early and late adolescence: Age and school climate effects. *Journal of Research on Adolescence*, 20(3), 748–773. doi:10.1111/j.1532-7795.2010.00658.x

Fletcher, G. J. O., Simpson, J. A., Thomas, G., & Giles, L. (1999). Ideals in intimate relationships. *Journal, of Personality and Social Psychology*, 76(4), 72–89. doi:http://dx.doi.org/10.1037/0022-3514.58.2.281

Franklin, K. M., Janoff-Bulman, R., & Roberts, J. E. (1990). Long-term impact of parental divorce on optimism and trust: Changes in general assumptions or narrow beliefs? *Journal of Personality and Social Psychology*, 59, 743–755. doi:http://dx.doi.org/10.1037/0022-3514.59.4.743

Fuertes, J. N., Toporovsky, A., Reyes, M., & Osborne, J. B. (2017, April). The physician-patient working alliance: Theory, research, and future possibilities. *Patient Education and Counseling*, 100(4), 610–615. doi:10.1016/j.pec.2016.10.018

Garen, J., & Clark, J. R. (2015). Trust and the growth of government. *CATO Journal*, 35(3), 549–580.

Gervais, J., Tremblay, R. E., & Desmarais-Gervais, L. (2000). Children's persistent lying, gender differences, and disruptive behaviours: A longitudinal perspective. *International Journal of Behavioral Development*, 24(2), 213–221. doi:10.1080/016502500383340

Goldsmith, A. (2005). Police reform and the problem of trust. *Theoretical Criminology*, 9, 443–470.

Granqvist, P., Mikulincer, M., Gewirtz, V., & Shaver, P. R. (2012). Experimental findings on God as an attachment figure: Normative processes and moderating effects of internal working models. *Journal of Personality and Social Psychology*, 103(5), 804–818. doi:10.1037/a0029344

Guardian News. (2015). The counted police killings. Retrieved from www.theguardian.com/us-news/ng-interactive/2015/jun/01/the-counted-police-killings-us-database

Guardian News. (2016). Police will be required to report officer-involved deaths under new US system. Retrieved from www.theguardian.com/us-news/2016/aug/08/police-officer-related-deaths-department-of-justice.

Hafizi, S., Rosmarin, D. H. G., & Koenig, H. (2014). Brief trust/mistrust in God scale: Psychometric properties of the Farsi version in Muslims. *Mental Health, Religion & Culture*, 17(4), 415–420. doi:10.1080/13674676.2013.816942

Hall, K., & Brosnan, S. F. (2017). Cooperation and deception in primates. *Infant Behavior & Development*. Part A, 48, 38–44. doi: http://dx.doi.org/10.1016/j.infbeh.2016.11.007

Hamachek, D. (1990). Evaluating self-concept and ego status in Erikson's last three psychosocial stages. *Journal of Counseling and Development, 68*(6), 677–683.

Hannon, P. A., Rusbult, C. E., Finkel, E. J., & Kamashiro, M. (2010). In the wake of betrayal, forgiveness, and the resolution of betrayal. *Personal Relationships, 17,* 253–278. doi:10.1111/j.1475-6811.2010.01275.x

Harding, A. (2014, October). *American's trust in doctors is failing.* Retrieved from www.livescience.com/48407-americans-trust-doctors-falling.html

Harris, P. L. (2007). Trust. *Developmental Science, 10*(1), 135–138. doi:0.1111/j.1467-7687.2007.00575.x

Hauch, V., Blandón-Gitlin, I., Masip, J., & Sporer, S. L. (2015). Are computers effective lie detectors? A meta-analysis of linguistic cues to deception. *Personality and Social Psychology Review, 19,* 307–342. doi:10.1177/1088868314556539

Hays, C., & Carver, L. (2014). Follow the liar: The effects of adult lies on children's honesty. *Developmental Science, 17*(6), 977–983. doi: 10.1111/desc.12171

Hazen, C., & Shaver, P. (1987). Romantic love conceptualised as an attachment process. *Journal of Personality and Social Psychology, 52*(3), 511–524. Merriam-Webster dictionary. Retrieved from www.merriam-webster.com/diction ary/trust

Hetherington, M. J., & Rudolph, T. J. (2008). Priming, performance, and the dynamics of political trust. *Journal of Politics, 70,* 498–512.

Hewstone, M. (2015). Consequences of diversity for social cohesion and preju-dice: The missing dimension of intergroup contact. *Journal of Social Issues, 71*(2), 417–438. doi:10.1111/josi.12120

Hruby, A., & Hu, F. (2015). The epidemiology of obesity: A big picture *Pharmaco Economics, 33*(7), 673–689. doi:10.1007/s40273-014-0243-x

Isotalus, P., & Almonkari, M. (2014). Political scandal tests trust in politicians. *Nordicom Review, 35*(2), 3–16. doi:10.2478/nor-2014-0011

Ivković, S. K., Peacock, R., & Haberfeld, M. (2016). Does discipline fairness mat-ter for the police code of silence? Answers from the US supervisors and line officers. *Policing: An International Journal of Police Strategies & Management, 39*(2), 354–369. doi:http://dx.doi.org/10.1108/PIJPSM-10-2015-0120

James, E. L. (2011). *Fifty shades of grey.* New York: Vintage Books.

Jamison, G. D. (2011). Interpersonal trust in Latin America: Analyzing variations in trust using data from the Latinobarómetro. *Journal of Multidisciplinary Research (1947–2900), 3*(3), 65–80.

Jensen, L., Arnett, J., Feldman, S., & Cauffman, E. (2004). The right to do wrong: Lying to parents among adolescents and emerging adults. *Journal of Youth and Adolescence*, 33(2), 101–112.

Jones, W. H., Chan, M. G., & Miller, C. E. (1991). Betrayal among children and adults. In K. J. Rotenberg (Ed.), *Children's interpersonal trust: Sensitivity to lying, deception, and promise violations* (pp. 118–134). New York: Spring-Verlag.

Kääriäinen, J. T. (2007). Trust in the police in 16 European countries: A multilevel analysis. *European Journal of Criminology*, 4(4), 409–435. doi:10.1177/147737080720

Kashy, D. A., & DePaulo, B. M. (1996). Who lies? *Journal of Personality and Social Psychology*, 70(5), 1037–1051.

Katz, W. (2015). Enhancing accountability and trust with independent investigations of police lethal force. *Harvard Law Review*, 128(6), 235–245.

Keelan, J. P. R., Dion, K. L., & Dion, K. K. (1994). Attachment style and heterosexual relationships among young adults: A short-term panel study. *Journal of Social and Personal Relationships*, 11(2), 201–214. doi:http://dx.doi.org/10.1177/0265407594112003

Kerns, K. A., Klepac, L., & Cole, A. K. (1996). Peer relationships and preadolescents' perceptions of security in the mother-child relationship. *Developmental Psychology*, 32(3), 457–456. doi:http://dx.doi.org/10.1037/0012-1649.32.3.457

Kerr, M., Stattin, H., & Trost, K. (1999). To know you is to trust you: Parents' trust is rooted in child disclosure of information. *Journal of Adolescence* 22(6), 737–752. doi: http://dx.doi.org/10.1006/jado.1999.0266

Kirkpatrick, L. A. (1992). An attachment-theory approach to the psychology of religion. *The International Journal for the Psychology of Religion*, 2, 3–28. doi:10.1207/s15327582ijpr0201_2

Kirkpatrick, L. A., & Davis, K. E. (1994). Attachment style, gender, and relationship stability: A longitudinal analysis. *Journal of Personality & Social Psychology*, 66(3), 502–512. doi:10.1037/0022-3514.66.3.502

Kolbert, E. (2016, November 3). How can Americans trust Donald Trump? *The New Yorker*. Retrieved from www.newyorker.com/news/daily-comment/how-can-americans-trust-donald-trump

Laughton-Brown, H. (2010). Trust in the therapeutic relationship: Psychodynamic contributions to counselling psychology practice. *Counselling Psychology Review*, 25, 12–17.

Lee, K. (2013). Little liars: Development of verbal deception in children. *Child Development Perspectives*, 7, 91–96. doi:10.1111/cdep.12023

Leigh, A. (2002). Explaining distrust: Popular attitudes towards politicians in Australia and the United States. In D. Burchell & A. Leigh (Eds.), *The Prince's new clothes: Why do Australians dislike their politicians?* Sydney: UNSW Press.

Levine, E. E. & Schweitzer, Maurice E. (2014). Are liars ethical? On the tension between benevolence and honesty. *Journal of Experimental Social Psychology*, 53, 107–117. doi: http://dx.doi.org/10.1016/j.jesp.2014.03.005

Lewis, M., Stanger, C., & Sullivan, M. W. (1989). Deception in 3-year olds. *Developmental Psychology*, 25, 439–443.

Lindskold, S. (1978). Trust development, the GRIT proposal, and the effects of conciliatory acts on conflict and cooperation. *Psychological Bulletin*, 85(4), 772–793. doi:http://dx.doi.org/10.1037/0033-2909.85.4.772

Luchies, L. B., Wieselquist, J., Rusbult, C. E., Kumashiro, M., Eastwick, P. W., Coolsen, M. K., & Finkel, E. J. (2013). Trust and biased memory of transgressions in romantic relationships. *Journal of Personality & Social Psychology*, 104(4), 673–694. doi:10.1037/a0031054

MacDonald, J., & Stokes, R. J. (2006). Race, social capital, and trust in the police. *Urban Affairs Review*, 41(3), 358–375. doi:10.1177/1078087405281707

Malti, T., Averdijk, M., Ribeaud, D., Eisner, M. P., & Rotenberg, K. J. (2013). Children's trust and developmental trajectories of aggressive behavior in an ethnically diverse sample. *Journal of Abnormal Child Psychology*, 41, 445–456.

Mark, K. P., Janssen, E., & Milhausen, R. R. (2011). Infidelity in heterosexual couples: Demographic, interpersonal, and personality-related predictors of extradyadic sex. *Archives of Sexual Behavior*, 40(5), 971–982. doi:10.1007/s10508-011-9771-z

Marschall, M. J., & Stolle, D. (2004). Race and the city: Neighborhood context and the development of generalized Trust. *Political Behavior*, 26(2), 125–153.

Marshall, T. C., Bejanyan, K., Di Castro, G., & Lee, R. A. (2013). Attachment styles as predictors of Facebook-related jealousy and surveillance in romantic relationships. *Personal Relationships*, 20(1), 1–22. doi:10.1111/j.1475-6811.2011.01393.x

Martin, A. (2010). Does political trust matter? Examining some of the implications of low levels of political trust in Australia. *Australian Journal of Political Science*, 45, 705–712. doi:10.1080/10361146.2010.517184

Mayer, R. C., & Davis, J. H. (1999). The effect of the performance appraisal system on trust for management: A field quasi-experiment. *Journal of Applied Psychology*, 84(1), 123–136. doi:http://dx.doi.org/10.1037/0021-9010.84.1.123

Mayer, R. C., Davis, J. H., & Schoorman, D. F. (1995). An integration model of organizational trust: *Academic Management Review*, 20, 709–735. doi:http://dx.doi.org/10.2307/258792

McEvily, B., Perrone, V., & Zaheer, A. (Eds.). (2003). Trust as an organizing principle. In special issue: Trust in an organizational content. *Organization Science*, 14, 91–103.

McNamara, J. D. (2012, March 15). Trust in American police remains high: Here's why. Delivered at the *50th Anniversary Law Enforcement Event*, San Francisco Bay Chapter, American Society of International Security, Foster City, CA.

Mekawi, Y., & Bresin, K. (2015). Is the evidence from racial bias shooting task studies a smoking gun? Results from a meta-analysis. *Journal of Experimental Social Psychology*, 61, 120–130. doi:10.1016/j.jesp.2015.08.002

Mikulincer, M. (1998). Attachment working models and the sense of trust: An exploration of interaction goals and affect regulation. *Journal of Personality and Social Psychology*, 74, 1209–1224.

Mirror News (2016). *Doctor conned out of £150,000 by fraudster she met online forced to sell home amid staggering debts.* Retrieved October 12, 2016, from www.mirror.co.uk/tv/tv-news/doctor-conned-out-150000-fraudster- 8537144.

Misztal, B. A. (1996). *Trust in Modern Societies.* Cambridge: Polity Press.

Moltmann, J. (2006). Control is good – trust is better. *Theology Today*, 62(4), 465–475.

Montague, P. R., King-Casas, B., & Cohen, T. D. (2006). Imagining valuation models in human choice. *Annual Review of Neuroscience*, 29, 417–448. doi:10.11416//neuro.29.051605.11903.

Murray, S. L., & Holmes, J. G. (2009). The architecture of interdependent minds: A motivation-management theory of mutual responsiveness. *Psychological Review*, 116(4), 908–928. doi:10.1037/a0017015

Northrup, C., Schwartz, P., & Witte, J. (2013). *The Normal Bar.* New York: Harmony, an Imprint of the Crown Publishing Group.

Nummela, O., Raivio, R., & Uutela, A. (2012). Trust, self-rated health and mortality: A longitudinal study among ageing people in Southern Finland.

Social Science & Medicine, 74(10), 1639–1643. doi http://dx.doi.org/10.1016/j.socscimed.2012.02.010

O'Hara, K. (2004). *Trust: From Socrates to spin.* Duxford, Cambridge: Cambridge University Press distributed by Icon Books.

Olson, D., & Miao, L. (2015). Does a nation's religious composition affect generalized trust? The role of religious heterogeneity and the percent religious. *Journal for the Scientific Study of Religion*, 54(4), 756–773. doi:10.1111/jssr.12231

Ortega, A., Brenner, S., & Leather, P. (2007). Occupational stress, coping and personality in the police: An SEM study. *International Journal of Police Science & Management*, 9, 36–50.

Osgood, C. E. (1962). *An alternative to war or surrender.* Urbana, IL: University of Illinois Press.

Paillé, P., Bourdeau, L., & Galois, I. (2010). Support, trust, satisfaction, intent to leave and citizenship at organizational level: A social exchange approach. *International Journal of Organizational Analysis*, 18, 41–45. doi:http://dx.doi.org/10.1108/19348831011033203

Papadopoulos, S., & Brennan, L. (2015). Correlates of weight stigma in adults with overweight and obesity: A systematic literature review. *Obesity*, 23(9), 1743–1760. doi:http://dx.doi.org/10.1002/oby.21187

Perrin, A. J., & Smolek, S. (2009). Who trusts? Race, gender and the September 11 rally effect among young adults. *Social Science Research*, 38(1), 134–145. doi:10.1016/j.ssresearch.2008.09.001

Peterson, C. C., Peterson, J. L., & Seeto, D. (1983). Developmental changes in ideas about lying *Child Development*, 54, 1529–1535. doi:10.1111/1467-8624.ep12418537

Pettigrew, T. F. (1998). Intergroup contact theory. *Annual Review of Psychology*, 49(1), 65–85.

Piaget, J. (1965). *The moral judgment of the child* (M. Gabain, Trans.). Glencoe, IL: Free Press. (Original work published 1932)

Pilgrim, D., Tomasini, F., & Vassilev, I. (2010). *Examining trust in healthcare: A multidisciplinary perspective.* London: Palgrave Macmillan.

Porter, L. E., & Warrender, C. (2009). A multivariate model of police deviance: Examining the nature of corruption, crime, and misconduct. *Policing & Society*, 19, 79–99.

Prall, D. (2014, December 22). Americans' trust in police average for developed countries. *American City & County Exclusive Insight.* Retrieved from http://americancityandcounty.com/law-enforcement/americans-trust-police-average-developed-countries

Qualter, P., Brown, S. L., Rotenberg, K. J., Vanhalst, J., Harris, R. A., Goossens, L., Bangee, M., & Munn, P. (2013). Trajectories of loneliness during childhood and adolescence: Predictors and health outcomes. *Journal of Adolescence: Special Issue on Loneliness,* 36, 1283–1293. doi:http://dx.doi.org/10.1016/j.adolescence.2013.01.005

Reifman, A., Villa, L. C., Amans, J. A., Rethinam, V., & Telesca, T. Y. (2001). Children of divorce in the 1990s: A meta-analysis. *Journal of Divorce and Remarriage,* 36, 27–36. doi:http://dx.doi.org/10.1300/J087v36n01_02

Rempel, J. K., Holmes, J. G., & Zanna, M. P. (1985). Trust in close relationships. *Journal of Personality and Social Psychology,* 49(1), 95–112.

Rempel, J. K., Ross, M., & Holmes, J. G. (2001). Trust and communicated attributions in close relationships. *Journal of Personality & Social Psychology,* 81(1), 57–64. doi:10.1037//0022-3514.81.1.57.

Rosmarin, D. H., Krumrei, E. J., & Andersson, G. (2009). Religion as a predictor of psychological distress in two religious communities. *Cognitive Behaviour Therapy,* 38, 54–64. doi:10.1080/16506070802477222

Rosmarin, D. H., Pargament, K. I., & Mahoney, A. (2009). The role of religiousness in anxiety, depression and happiness in a Jewish community sample: A preliminary investigation. *Mental Health Religion and Culture,* 12(2), 97–113. doi:10.1080/13674670802321933

Rosmarin, D. H., Pargament, K. I., Pirutinsky, S., & Mahoney, A. (2010). A randomized controlled evaluation of a spiritually integrated treatment for subclinical anxiety in the Jewish community, delivered via the Internet. *Journal of Anxiety Disorders,* 24(7), 799–808. doi:10.1016/j.janxdis.2010.05.014

Rosmarin, D. H., Pargament, K. I., & Robb, H. (2010). Introduction to special series: Spiritual and religious issues in behavior change. *Cognitive and Behavioral Practice,* 17(4), 343–347. doi:http://dx.doi.org/10.1016/j.cbpra.2009.02.007

Rosmarin, D. H., Pirutinsky, S., & Pargament, K. I. (2011). A brief measure of core religious beliefs for use in psychiatric settings. *International Journal of Psychiatry in Medicine,* 41(3), 253–261. doi:http://dx.doi.org/10.2190/PM.41.3.d

Rostila, M. (2010). The facets of social capital. *Journal for the Theory of Social Behaviour,* 41(3), 307–327.

Rotenberg, K. J. (1991). Children's cue use and strategies for detecting deception. In K. J. Rotenberg (Ed.), *Children's interpersonal trust: Sensitivity to lying, deception and promise violations* (pp. 43–57). New York: Springer-Verlag.

Rotenberg, K. J. (1995). The socialisation of trust: Parents' and children's interpersonal trust. *International Journal of Behavioral Development,* 18, 713–726.

Rotenberg, K. J. (2010). The conceptualization of interpersonal trust: A basis, domain, and target framework. In K. J. Rotenberg (Ed.), *Interpersonal trust during childhood and adolescence* (pp. 8–27). New York: Cambridge University Press.

Rotenberg, K. J. (2015). Trust across the life-span. In N. J. Smelser & P. B. Baltes (Eds.), *International encyclopedia of the social & behavioral sciences* (pp. 866–868). New York: Pergamon.

Rotenberg, K. J. (2016, June 13). The EU referendum: It is a matter of trust. *Conversations.*

Rotenberg, K. J., Addis, N., Betts, L. R., Fox, C., Hobson, Z., Rennison, S., Trueman, M., & Boulton, M. J. (2010). The relation between trust beliefs and loneliness during early childhood, middle childhood and adulthood. *Personality and Psychosocial Psychology Bulletin,* 36, 1086–1100. doi:http://dx.doi.org/10.1177/0146167210374957

Rotenberg, K. J., Betts, L. R., Eisner, M., & Ribeaud, D. (2012). Social antecedents of children's trustworthiness. *Infant and Child Development,* 21, 310–322. doi:10.1002/icd.751

Rotenberg, K. J., Bharathi, C., Davies, H., & Finch, T. (2013). Bulimic symptoms and the social withdrawal syndrome. *Eating Behaviors,* 14(3), 281–284. doi:http://dx.doi.org/10.1016/j.eatbeh.2013.05.003

Rotenberg, K. J., Bharathi, C., Davies, H., & Finch, T. (2017). Obesity and the social withdrawal syndrome. *Eating Behaviors,* 26, 167–170. doi: org/10.1016/j.eatbeh.2017.03.006

Rotenberg, K. J., & Bierbrauer, T. (in preparation). Development of a new trust in politicians scale: Its relationship with Voting in the UK.

Rotenberg, K. J., Boulton, M. J., & Fox, C. (2005). Cross-sectional and longitudinal relations among trust beliefs, psychological maladjustment, and psychosocial relationships, during childhood: Are very high as well as very low trusting children at risk? *Journal of Abnormal Child Psychology,* 33, 595–610. doi:http://dx.doi.org/10.1007/s10802-005-6740-9

Rotenberg, K. J., & Cerda, C. (1994). Racially based trust expectancies of Native American and Caucasian children. *Journal of Social Psychology*, 134, 621–631.

Rotenberg, K. J., Cunningham, J., Hayton, N., Hutson, L., Jones, L., Marks, C. Woods, E., & Betts, L. R. (2008). Development of a children's trust in general physicians scale. *Child: Health, Care and Development*, 34, 748–756. doi:10.1111/j.1365-2214.2008.00872.x

Rotenberg, K. J., Fox, C., Green, S., Ruderman, L., Slater, K., Stevens, K., & Carlo, G. (2005). Construction and validation of a children's interpersonal trust belief scale. *British Journal of Developmental Psychology*, 23, 271–292. doi:10.1348/026151005X26192

Rotenberg, K. J., Harrison, A., & Reeves, C. (2016). The relations between police officers' personal trust beliefs in the police and their workplace adjustment. *Policing and Society*, 26, 627–641. doi:10.1080/10439463.2014.100 0324.

Rotenberg, K. J., Petrocchi, S., Lecciso, F., & Marchetti, A. (2013). Children's trust beliefs and trusting behavior. *Child Development Research*, Article ID 806597, 8 pages.

Rotenberg, K. J., Qualter, P., Barrett, L., & Henzi, P. (2014). When trust fails: Children's trust beliefs in peers and peer interactions in a natural setting. *Journal of Abnormal Child Psychology*, 42, 967–980. doi:http://dx.doi. org/10.1007/s10802-013-9835-8

Rotenberg, K. J., & Sangha, R. (2015). Bulimic symptoms and social withdrawal during early adolescence. *Eating Behaviors*, 19, 177–180. doi:http://dx.doi. org/10.1016/j.eatbeh.2015.09.008

Rotenberg, K. J., Woods, E., & Betts, L. R. (2015). Development of a scale to assess children's trust in general nurses. *Journal of Specialists in Pediatric Nursing*, 20(4), 298–303. doi:10.1111/jspn.12126

Rotter, J. B. (1967). A new scale for the measurement of interpersonal trust. *Journal of Personality*, 35, 651–665.

Rotter, J. B. (1980). Interpersonal trust, trustworthiness and gullibility. *American Psychologist*, 35, 1–7. doi:http://dx.doi.org/10.1037/0003-066X.35.1.1

Saha, S., Jacobs, E. A., Moore, R. D., & Beach, M. C. (2010). Trust in physicians and racial disparities in HIV care. *AIDS Patient Care and STDs*, 24(7), 415–420. doi:10.1089/apc.2009.0288

Schiffman, L., Thelen, S. T., & Sherman, E. (2010). Interpersonal and political trust: Modeling levels of citizens' trust. *European Journal of Marketing*, 44(3/4), 369–381.doi:10.1108/03090561011020471

Schneider, B. H., Atkinson, L., & Tardif, C. (2001). Child – parent attachment and children's peer relations: A quantitative review. *Developmental Psychology*, 37(1), 86–100. doi:http://dx.doi.org/10.1037/0012-1649.37.1.86

Schneider, I. K., Konijn, E. A., Righetti, F., & Rusbult, C. E. (2011). A healthy dose of trust: The relationship between interpersonal trust and health. *Personal Relationships*, 18(4), 668–676. doi:10.1111/j.1475-6811.2010.01338.x

Schoorman, F. D., Mayer, R. C., & Davis, J. H. (2007). An integrative model of organizational trust: Past, present, and future. *The Academy of Management Review*, 32(2), 344–354. doi:http://dx.doi.org/10.2307/20159304

Semukhina, O., & Reynolds, K. M. (2014). Russian citizens' perceptions of corruption and trust of the police. *Policing & Society*, 24(2), 158–188. doi:10.1080/10439463.2013.784290

Serota, K. B., Levine, T. R., & Boster, F. J. (2010). The prevalence of lying in America: Three studies of self-reported lies. *Human Communication Research*, 36, 2–25. doi:10.1111/j.1468-2958.2009.01366.x

Shackelford, T. K., Buss, D. M., & Bennett, K. (2002). Forgiveness or breakup: Sex differences in responses to a partner's infidelity. *Cognition & Emotion*, 16(2), 299–307. doi:10.1080/02699930143000202

Shallcross, S. I., & Simpson, J. (2012). Trust and responsiveness in strain-test situations: A dyadic process. *Journal of Personality and Social Psychology*, 102(5), 1031–1044. doi:10.1037/a0026829

Shiri, E., & Bruce, M. H. (2008). Tell-tale eyes: Children's attribution of gaze aversion as a lying cue. *Developmental Psychology*, 44(6), 1655–1667. doi:10.1037/a0013299

Sholihin, M., & Pike, R. (2010). Organisational commitment in the police service: Exploring the effects of performance measures, procedural justice and interpersonal trust. *Financial Accountability & Management*, 26, 392–342.

Skocpol, T. (2002). Will 9/11 and the war on terror revitalize American civic democracy. *PS: Political Science and Politics*, 35, 537–540.

Slack, J. (2016, October 6). Britain 'is suffering a huge loss of faith in its institutions'. Retrieved November 4, 2016, from www.dailymail.co.uk/news/article-2296085. (Originally PUBLISHED: 00:26, March 20, 2013 | UPDATED: 07:42, March 20, 2013.

Smith, B., & Steel, C. (2009). 'Suspicion is my friend': Cognitive behavioural therapy for post-traumatic persecutory delusions. In N. Grey (Ed.), *A casebook of cognitive therapy for traumatic stress reactions* (pp. 61–77). New York: Routledge/Taylor & Francis Group.

Stice, E., Marti, N., & Rohde, P. (2013). Prevalence, incidence, impairment, and course of the proposed DSM-5 eating disorder diagnoses in an 8-year prospective community study of young women. *Journal of Abnormal Psychology, 122*(2), 445–457. doi:http://dx.doi.org/10.1037/a0030679

Sun, Y., & Li, Y. (2002). Children's well-being during parents' marital disruption process: A pooled time-series analysis. *Journal of Marriage and Family, 64,* 472–488.

Sunshine, J., & Tyler, T. R. (2003). The role of procedural justice and legitimacy in shaping public support for policing. *Law and Society Review, 17,* 513–547.

Swami, V., Chamorro-Premuzic, T., & Furnham, A. (2010). Unanswered questions: A preliminary investigation of personality and individual difference predictors of 9/11 conspiracist beliefs. *Applied Cognitive Psychology, 24*(6), 749–761. doi:10.1002/acp.1583

Tajfel, H. (1981). *Human groups and social categories: Studies in social psychology.* Cambridge, MA: Cambridge University Press.

Talwar, V., & Crossman, A. (2011). From little white lies to filthy liars: The evolution of honesty and deception in young children. *Advances in Child Development & Behavior, 40,* 139–179.

Talwar, V., & Lee, K. (2008). Social and cognitive correlates of children's lying behavior. *Child Development, 79*(4), 866–888. doi:10.1111/j.1467-8624.2008.01164.x

Tam, T., Hewstone, M., Kenworthy, J., & Cairns, E. (2009). Intergroup trust in Northern Ireland. *Personality & Social Psychology Bulletin, 35*(1), 45–59. doi:http://dx.doi.org/10.1177/0146167208325004

Tan, H. H., & Lim, A. H. (2009). Trust in coworkers and trust in organizations. *The Journal of Psychology, 143*(1), 45–66.

Thom, D. H., Kravitz, R. L., Bell, R. A., Krupat, E., & Azari, R. (2002). Patient trust in the physician: Relationship to patient requests. *Family Practice, 19*(5), 476–483.

Thom, D. H., Ribisl, K. M., Stewart, A. L., Luke, D. A., & The Stanford Trust Study Physicians. (1999). Further validation and reliability testing of the trust in physician scale. *Medical Care, 37*(5), 510–517.

Thompson, M., & Kahn, K. B. (2016). Mental health, race, and police contact: Intersections of risk and trust in the police. *Policing: An International Journal, 39*(4), 807–819. doi:10.1108/PIJPSM-02-2016-0015

Thorne, B. (2007). Person-centred therapy. In W. Dryden (Ed.), *Dryden's handbook of individual therapy* (5th ed., pp. 144–172). Thousand Oaks, CA: Sage Publications.

Trinkner, R., Tyler, T. R., & Goff, P. A. (2016). Justice from within: The relations between a procedurally just organizational climate and police organizational efficiency, endorsement of democratic policing, and officer wellbeing. *Psychology, Public Policy, and Law*, 22(2), 158–172. doi:10.1177/174 8895814566288

Turner, J. C., Hogg, M. A., Oakes, P. J., Reicher, S. D., & Wetherell, M. S. (1987). *Rediscovering the social group: A self-categorization theory*. Cambridge, MA: Basil Blackwell.

Turner, R. H., Hewstone, M., Swart, H., Tam, T., Myers, E., & Tausch, N. (2010). Promoting intergroup trust among adolescents and among adults. In K. J. Rotenberg (Ed.), *Interpersonal trust during childhood and adolescence* (pp. 295–321). Cambridge: Cambridge University Press.

Turner, R. N., Tam, T., Hewstone, M., Kenworthy, J., & Cairns, E. (2013). Contact between Catholic and Protestant schoolchildren in Northern Ireland. *Journal of Applied Social Psychology*, 43(Suppl 2), E216–E228. doi:http://dx.doi.org/10.1111/jasp.12018

Tyler, T. R. (2001). Public trust and confidence in legal authorities: What do majority and minority group members want from the law and legal institutions? *Behavioral Sciences & the Law*, 19(2), 215–235. doi:http://dx.doi.org/10.1002/bsl.438

Tyler, T. R. (2015). Why trust matters with juveniles. *American Journal of Orthopsychiatry*, 85(6, Suppl), Special Issue: Finding Meaning in Community: Trust in and by Young People, 93–9.

Tyler, T. R., & Huo, Y. J. (2002). *Trust in the law: Encouraging public cooperation with the police and courts*. New York: Russell Sage Foundation.

Uslander, E. M. (2002). *The moral foundations of trust*. Cambridge: Cambridge University Press.

Video of Black Man Shoot by Police. (2016). Retrieved November 7, 2016, from www.theguardian.com/us- news/2016/jul/07/facebook-live-video-appears-to-show-black-man-shot-police-minnesota-philando-castile; *Washington Post*, www.washingtonpost.com/graphics/national/police-shootings-2016/

Voci, A. (2006). The link between identification and in-group favouritism: Effects of threat to social identity and trust-related emotions. *British Journal of Social Psychology*, 45(2), 265–284. doi:10.1348/014466605X52245

Walia, A. (2015, May 23). Editor in chief of world's best known medical journal: Half of all the literature is false. *Global Research*. Retrieved from www.globalresearch.ca /5451305.

Ward, P. R., Mamerow, L., & Meyer, S. B. (2014). Interpersonal trust across six Asia-pacific countries: Testing and extending the 'High Trust Society' and 'Low Trust Society' theory. *Plos One*, 9(4),1–17. doi: 10.1371/journal.pone.0095555

Warneken, F., & Orlins, E. (2015). Children tell white lies to make others feel better. *British Journal of Developmental Psychology*, 33(3), 259–270. doi:10.1111/bjdp.12083.

Warren, M. E. (Ed.). (1999). *Democracy and trust*. New York and Cambridge: Cambridge University Press.

Warren, M. E. (2004). What does corruption mean in a democracy? *American Journal of Political Science*, 48(2), 328–343.

Waters, E., & Deane, K. (1985). Defining and assessing individual differences in attachment relationships: Q-methodology and organization of behaviour in infancy and early childhood. *Monographs of the Society for Research in Child Development*, 50(1/2), 41–65.

Westermarland, L. (2005). Police ethics and integrity: Breaking the blue code of silence. *Policing & Society*, 15, 145–165.

Williams, K. (2010). Police violence, resistance, crisis of legitmacy: Politics of Killer Cops and Cop Killers. *Against the Current*, 25–29.

Woods, J. (2011). The 9/11 effect: Toward a social science of the terrorist threat. *The Social Science Journal*, 48(1), 1–21.

Xu, F. Bao, X., Fu, G., Bao, X., Fu. G., Talwar, V., & Lee, K. (2010). Lying and truth-telling in children: from concept to action. *Child Development*, 81(2): 581–596. http://dx.doi.org/10.1111/j.1467-8624.2009.01417.x

Yan, L. L., Daviglus, M. L., Liu, K., Pirzada, A., Garside, D. B., Schiffer, L., Dyer, A. R., & Greenland, P. (2004). BMI and health-related quality of life in adults 65 years and older. *Obesity Research*, 12(1), 69–76.

Zizumbo-Colunga, D., Zechmeister, E. J., & Seligso, M. A. (2010). Social capital and economic Crisis in the United States. *Americas Barometer Insights*, No. 43, Vanderbilt University. Retrieved from www.vanderbilt.edu/lapop/insights/I0843en.pdf

Printed in the United States
by Baker & Taylor Publisher Services